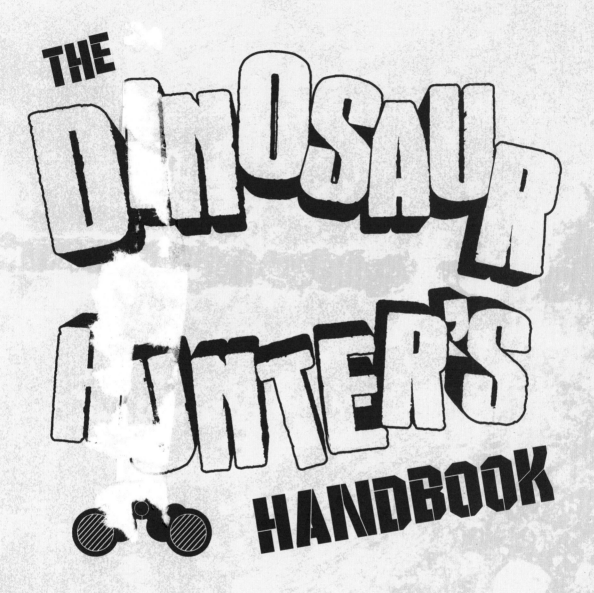

THE DINOSAUR HUNTER'S HANDBOOK

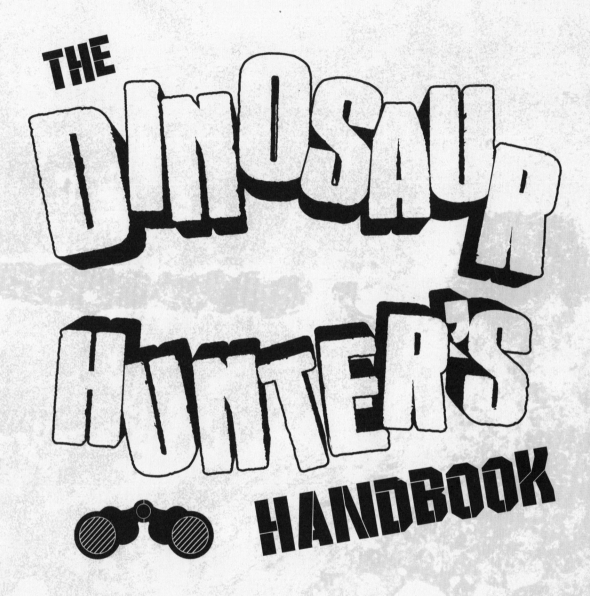

THE DINOSAUR HUNTER'S HANDBOOK

SCOTT FORBES

CARLTON
KiDS

CONT

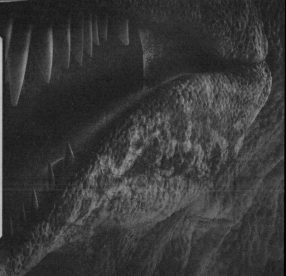

ENTS

HUNTING FOR DINOSAURS

Ready for adventure? You're going on a trip back in time to view some of the most awesome animals ever to roam our planet: the dinosaurs. You'll travel the world, fight your way through forests, wade across rivers and swamps, climb hills and mountains, and trek across baking hot deserts. And you'll meet more than 50 different kinds of dinosaurs, ranging from cute little feathered reptiles no bigger than a chicken to some of the largest and most terrifying creatures that have ever lived.

To prepare for your trip, read our guide to *the world of dinosaurs*, starting on page 8. There, you'll learn about types of dinosaurs and what they ate, their strengths and weaknesses, their battles and their babies, and how we have learned so much about them.

Once you're on your way, our handy *Spotter's Guide*, starting on page 24, will tell you what to look for, where to find it and how to identify it. The guide will also help you steer clear of danger and, most importantly, avoid becoming a swift and no doubt tasty snack for a hungry predator!

Now grab your gear, and get ready to go!

THE WORLD OF DINOSAURS

WHEN DINOSAURS RULED

Dinosaurs roamed Earth for 160 million years, from around 235 to 66 million years ago. That span of time is known as the Mesozoic Era and it is divided into three periods: the Triassic, Jurassic and Cretaceous. From a slow start in the middle of the Triassic Period, dinosaurs gradually spread far and wide, until there were dozens of kinds, or species, living all over the world.

Climate change

The Triassic was generally warm and dry. There were scattered forests of conifer trees, including ginkgo and monkey-puzzle trees (which are still around today), as well as palm-like cycads. There were ferns and mosses, but no grasses or flowers. The climate became wetter in the Jurassic, which helped plants grow taller and more thickly. The first flowering plants appeared in the Early Cretaceous. In the Late Cretaceous the climate cooled, creating wide, open plains covered with ferns and shrubs.

Fossils of ginkgo leaves beside a modern leaf

DINOSAUR TIMELINE

Our planet was constantly changing throughout the Mesozoic Era, and dinosaurs had to adapt to survive. They became so good at this that by the time of the Jurassic Period they were the biggest, strongest group of land animals on Earth.

Dinosaurs and mammals evolve

Birds evolve

TRIASSIC PERIOD	JURASSIC PERIOD	
252 mya	201 mya	145 mya

MESOZOIC ERA

CONTINENTAL DRIFT

During the Triassic Period, all of our planet's landmasses were joined together, forming one huge supercontinent, Pangaea. Animals could roam freely across this wide land. But during the Jurassic and Cretaceous, Pangaea split into smaller continents, each with different environments. As groups of dinosaurs adapted to their new surroundings, more and more species evolved.

TRIASSIC

Pangaea

CRETACEOUS

North America

Europe

Asia

South America

Africa

Australia

Antarctica

Golden age

The number of dinosaurs and dinosaur species reached a peak in the Late Cretaceous, between 83 and 70 million years ago, a time known as the Campanian age. There were up to 100 types of dinosaurs roaming the Earth then, including herds of big horned and crested plant-eaters that grazed on ferns and shrubs, as well as some giant, ferocious meat-eaters.

In fact, no other group of land animals has ruled our planet for so long. Even the mammals, the group that includes humans, have only dominated the animal kingdom for the last 66 million years.

Dinosaurs become extinct, but birds survive

Mammals become the dominant animals

Humans evolve

CRETACEOUS PERIOD

66 mya

Now

CENOZOIC ERA

FAMILY SNAPSHOT

Dinosaurs emerged out of a group of reptiles called archosaurs. This happened when some archosaurs developed different features from the others, eventually becoming another kind of animal altogether.

Reaching a length of up to 33m, Apatosaurus was one of the largest land animals that ever lived.

Shape shifting

Among the changes that made dinosaurs different from other reptiles were legs that extended straight down from the underside of the body rather than out to the side (like those of lizards today). This allowed dinosaurs to stand upright, which also meant they could move faster and breathe more easily.

Extra large

By making the most of their advantages over other animals, dinosaurs grabbed a larger share of available food supplies. This allowed them to dominate more and more environments and in turn grow in number, type and size.

One of the earliest dinosaurs discovered so far, Herrerasaurus was a two-legged South American meat-eater.

Reptile relatives

Other reptiles continued to live and flourish alongside the dinosaurs. Winged creatures called pterosaurs dominated the skies and marine reptiles, including plesiosaurs, pliosaurs and ichthyosaurs, swam the oceans. Many of these were massive. It must have been a scary world!

A pliosaur, Liopleurodon was one of the most fearsome sea predators of prehistoric times.

A colossal winged reptile, Quetzalcoatlus is the largest animal that ever took to the air!

FAMILY TREE

Early in their development, dinosaurs split into two groups, the saurischians (sore-ISS-key-ans) and the ornithischians (or-nith-ISS-key-ans). Within these two 'orders', as they are known, dinosaurs formed the following progressively smaller groups: sub-order, family, genus and species.

Ceratopsians Pachycephalosaurs

Ornithopods

Stegosaurs Ankylosaurs

Sauropods

Theropods

Herrerasaurids

SAURISCHIANS

ORNITHISCHIANS

DINOSAURS

The saurischians included the biggest dinosaurs, the mostly long-necked sauropods, and the fiercest, the meat-eating theropods.

Members of the ornithischian order included the spiky stegosaurs, horned ceratopsians and armoured ankylosaurs.

ON THE MENU

With plants and animals thriving throughout the Mesozoic Era, there was plenty of food around for the dinosaurs. Many became plant-eaters, or herbivores, others purely meat-eaters, or carnivores, while some, called omnivores, ate just about anything! Dinosaurs' bodies developed in different ways to suit their particular diets.

Strong growth

Some plant-eaters grew steadily bigger through the Late Triassic and Jurassic, so that they could reach higher into trees and further across the ground. This led to the emergence of the biggest, tallest dinosaurs ever: the sauropods. In the Late Cretaceous, large numbers of smaller (but still huge!) herbivores, including the duckbilled hadrosaurs and the horned ceratopsians, roamed in herds, grazing on ferns and shrubs.

Among ceratopsians like Triceratops males used their horns to fight rivals.

Sauropods like Brachiosaurus could eat up to 400kg of plants a day!

Down the hatch

Big sauropods like Brachiosaurus had peg-like teeth that were good for raking leaves off trees but useless for chewing. So they simply swallowed their food whole. To help them digest this coarse material, they also swallowed stones, known as gastroliths, which rolled around in their stomachs and mashed up the plant matter.

Chop and grind

Some of the smaller herbivores were equipped with jaws and teeth that helped them break down plant matter before swallowing it. The horned ceratopsians, like Triceratops, had hard, sharp-edged beaks that could slice through leaves and branches, and self-sharpening back teeth that then chopped this food into smaller pieces. The duckbilled hadrosaurs, such as Parasaurolophus, had rows of teeth for grinding plants into a paste. The uppermost rows of their teeth were constantly being replaced as they wore out.

Triceratops

Parasaurolophus

A TASTE FOR BLOOD

Carnivores either hunted other animals or scavenged dead meat, or did both. Some grew enormous. Hunting could be exhausting, but meat provided lots of energy, so that after a kill a hunter may not have to eat again for several days.

Spinosaurus could hunt on land and in shallow water.

Troodon caught small animals but also fed on leaves and fruit.

A varied diet

Many dinosaurs were omnivorous, nibbling on plants, guzzling up small creatures like insects and lizards, and scavenging on dead animals – often ones left by bigger hunters.

ATTACK AND DEFENCE

Carnivores developed a range of weapons and strategies to help them hunt and kill other creatures. In response, many herbivores evolved tough defences, including body armour, horns and spikes, and strong, whip-like tails.

DEADLY WEAPONS

Most meat-eaters had fairly large brains, good eyesight and a highly developed sense of smell. But their deadliest weapons were their sharp teeth, powerful jaws and deadly claws.

Some of the bigger carnivores such as Tyrannosaurus had a massive mouth full of humungous teeth – some as long as 30cm (including the root) – that could chomp straight through bone.

Edmontonia

Extra protection

Among smaller dinosaurs, the best forms of defence were hiding or running away – fast! But bigger herbivores, in particular, were too heavy and slow to escape. Some, like the giant sauropods, relied on their enormous size to scare off predators. Others, such as the rhino-like ankylosaurs and stegosaurs, were shielded by thick, bony, armour-like plates that covered their head, neck and back.

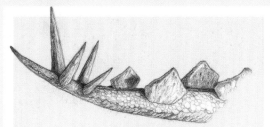

Stegosaurus tail

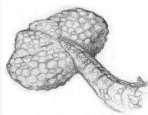

Euoplocephalus tail

Fighting back

When all else fails, fight back! Some big herbivores had their own secret weapons, most notably long tails that could be swung hard at an attacker. The tails of some ankylosaurs and stegosaurs were tipped with long, sharp spikes or heavy clubs. Some sauropods, such as Diplodocus, could crack their tails like whips, creating a deafening sound that scared off attackers.

This adult Tenontosaurus is trying in vain to shake off a pack of ferocious Deinonychus, which have already inflicted severe injuries.

On the prowl

Bigger hunters often stalked their victims alone, picking off easy kills such as young or sick dinosaurs, or charging out from hiding places to surprise larger targets. Smaller predators, such as Deinonychus, shown here, made up for what they lacked in size by hunting in packs. Working together, groups of Deinonychus could surround and kill animals much bigger than themselves.

EGGS AND NESTS

Like birds today, dinosaurs laid hard-shelled eggs, from which their babies hatched. While some dinosaurs carefully built mound-like nests, others simply plonked their eggs on the ground and covered them with a thin layer of sand or soil.

Breaking out

Dinosaur eggs were all shapes and sizes. Some were round like footballs, while others were oval or almost cylindrical. This baby Brachiosaurus is emerging from its mother's egg, which is round and about 30cm long and 20cm wide. Sauropods seem to have laid their eggs in piles on the ground, possibly buried under soil or sand.

Record nest

Large ostrich-like dinosaurs called oviraptors laid long, narrow eggs like these, measuring up to 30cm. They were placed in a circle on top of a mound of earth and may have been covered with dirt or foliage to keep them warm. One nest like this found in China was over 3m in diameter – almost as long as a small car – and contained 28 eggs, making it the biggest ever found.

Each of these eggs would have weighed about 5kg!

PARENTAL PRIORITIES

After laying, many dinosaurs abandoned their eggs. The babies would hatch out later and have to fend for themselves immediately. Others, like Psittacosaurus, shown here, remained with and cared for their young until they could walk and find food by themselves.

Groups of Psittacosaurus of different ages lived and foraged for food together.

In the nursery

Some species built clusters of nests in one place so that a group of parents could work together to protect their young against predators. This North American dinosaur, called Maiasaura, did this. It also seems to have lain on its nest until its young hatched out. Hence its name, which means 'good mother lizard'!

GONE IN A FLASH?

The dinosaur world came to a sudden end about 66 million years ago when, along with about 85 percent of all other living things, virtually all dinosaurs were wiped out. But, although you may not have noticed, some of their descendants are still around today.

Catastrophic collision

The main cause of the sudden loss of life – or mass extinction – that occurred 66 million years ago appears to have been an 11km wide asteroid that suddenly struck Earth. The vast crater formed by the asteroid was found off the coast of Mexico in 1990.

Bubbling up

The asteroid impact created a colossal explosion as well as earthquakes, which in turn caused widespread fires and tsunamis. At the same time there were huge volcanic eruptions in India. The air was filled with smoke, dust and poisonous gases. This blocked out the sun, destroying plants and making our planet much colder.

Survival strategies

The creatures that survived were mainly those that lived in the sea or in caves or could hide in holes or burrows. Among animals that lived in the open, only those that could move quickly to other environments to find food, such as birds, or ones that could eat a wide range of foods were able to survive.

DINOSAURS TODAY

Some reptiles lived through the mass extinction, including some lizards and crocodiles, and their descendants are still around. But though they look similar to dinosaurs, they are only distant relatives. The dinosaurs' most direct descendants – so closely related that they can be considered true dinosaurs – are, believe it or not, birds. You might look at these little feathery creatures quite differently now!

Yes, this is a real dinosaur!

21

SIGNS OF LIFE

How do we know so much about dinosaurs when they lived such a long time ago, long before humans made an appearance? The answer is fossils – remains of dinosaurs that have been found in the ground or imprinted on rocks.

Images of Archaeopteryx (left) are based on fossils like this one (right).

Set in stone

The most common types of fossils form when a creature dies and is buried by soil or sediments. Its softer body parts, such as flesh and organs, quickly waste away, but its harder parts, such as bones and teeth, may, over millions of years, be reinforced by minerals as the sediment turns to rock. The fossil remains may then be dug up, either deliberately or by chance. Fossilised dinosaur poos have also been found and are known as coprolites.

This Polacanthus fossil clearly shows the pattern on the dinosaur's skin.

Early impressions

Other kinds of fossils include impressions of plants and animals, formed as they pressed against soft soil or sediments that then turned to stone. These may show the outlines of dinosaurs, their skeletons or footprints, or even, in rare cases, the patterns on their skin.

Displays such as this Tyrannosaurus skeleton may be a combination of fossils and plaster models of bones.

Pieces of a puzzle

Scientists who study ancient creatures – known as palaeontologists (pah-lay-on-TAW-loh-jists) – can use fossilised bones and teeth to recreate the skeletons of dinosaurs and, based on that information, work out their muscle structure and the shape of their bodies. Fossilised footprints tell them more about how dinosaurs moved, and coprolites can reveal exactly what dinosaurs ate.

This engraving shows William Buckland at work in his study.

POINTING THE WAY

Almost certainly, people have been finding dinosaur fossils for thousands of years. But it wasn't until the 1800s that they realised what they were. In 1824, English scientist William Buckland decided that a fossilised jawbone came from an ancient giant lizard, which he named Megalosaurus. In 1842, after many similar fossils had been discovered, another English scientist, Richard Owen, coined a new name for such prehistoric reptiles: dinosaurs, meaning 'terrible lizards'.

SPOTTER'S GUIDE

AMARGASAURUS

Ah-marg-ah-SAW-rus

Name means: Lizard from La Amarga (town in Argentina where fossils were discovered)

This small South American sauropod is the porcupine of the dinosaur world, with numerous long spines lining its neck and back. As well as providing protection against predators, these attract mates and can be used to warn of approaching danger.

DANGER RATING: 3

- Long spikes on neck and back
- Small for a sauropod but could still be 100 times your weight!

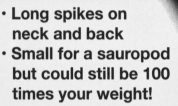

Argentina

RECORD BREAKER

Amargasaurus is the dinosaur with the spikiest neck. Several other species have spikes on various parts of their bodies but no other dinosaur has so many long, pointed spines running from its head along its back.

TRIASSIC PERIOD	JURASSIC PERIOD	
252 mya	201 mya	

MESOZOIC ERA

Early Cretaceous
130–125 million years ago

Spines continue along back but are covered with a large fold of skin, known as a sail

Horse-like head and peg-like teeth

Longest spines, in middle of neck, are up to 50cm long, with sharp points

SPOTTER STATS

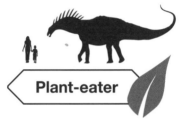

Plant-eater

Length:	13m
Weight:	4 tonnes
Speed:	16km/h
IQ:	Low
Sub-order:	Sauropodomorpha
Family:	Dicraeosauridae

Swallows stones (called gastroliths) to help mash up food in stomach

Walks on four legs and unable to rear up on two

WHERE TO LOOK?

Use binoculars to scan the sprawling South American woodlands, where these creatures like to graze on low-growing ferns and shrubs. Move towards them slowly, so as not to startle them. If they spot you, they may clack their spines together to try to scare you off.

AMPHICOELIAS

Am-fee-SEE-lee-us

Name means: Hollow on both sides (a reference to the structure of its bones)

It's a truly awesome sight: the biggest dinosaur you'll ever see! Even from kilometres away, it looks enormous, dwarfing everything around it. You'd barely reach its ankle. Lucky for you, this gentle giant is a plant-eater!

DANGER RATING:

4

- Colossal size – if it treads on you, you're a goner
- Swinging tail could knock you out

Bones contain numerous cavities to make them lighter

Gargantuan body needs hundreds of kilograms of food a day to power it

USA, Canada

Each leg is as tall as two giraffes standing on top of each other

TRIASSIC PERIOD	JURASSIC PERIOD	
252 mya	201 mya	145 mya

MESOZOIC ERA

Late Jurassic
155–145 million years ago

WHERE TO LOOK?

Amphicoelias roams the North American plains, gobbling up huge quantities of ferns and snacking on pockets of forest. Maybe the ground will tremble beneath your feet, or you'll see its giant neck and head rearing out of the trees – however you first sense it, it's likely to be from afar. Keep your distance and enjoy this astounding sight from a safe spot.

Narrow, pencil-shaped teeth used to rip out ferns and strip foliage off trees

Massive, flexible neck, long enough to reach the highest treetops

Enormous size of adult makes it almost impossible for a predator or even a group of predators to bring down

RECORD BREAKER

This is probably the biggest land animal that ever lived – longer than a blue whale, the biggest creature on Earth today, though not quite as heavy. Scientists aren't sure of its exact size, as it's very rare.

SPOTTER STATS

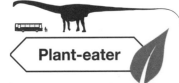

Plant-eater

Length:	Up to 60m
Weight:	Up to 120 tonnes
Speed:	16km/h
IQ:	Low
Sub-order:	Sauropodomorpha
Super-family:	Diplodocoidea

CRETACEOUS PERIOD

66 mya

CENOZOIC ERA

Now

ANCHIORNIS

An-kee-ORR-nis

Name means: Near bird

About the size of a pigeon, Anchiornis looks like a bird too: covered in feathers, with a crest and wide wings. But its broad, blunt snout, small teeth and stocky legs might have you wondering. And you'd be right to think twice: for Anchiornis is actually a small, feathered dinosaur.

Strong jaw with teeth for munching on lizards, insects and other small creatures

DANGER RATING:

1

- Sharp teeth, so it could give you a nip
- Long claws that can scratch skin
- Tiny though!

Long claws help with climbing trees and grasping prey

China

Large flight feathers on wings allow Anchiornis to glide short distances

TRIASSIC PERIOD	JURASSIC PERIOD	
252 mya	201 mya	145 mya

MESOZOIC ERA

Late Jurassic
165–155 million years ago

Bright red crest, used to attract a mate

Step silently through the north-eastern Chinese forests, trying not to create any loud noises. Peer into the trees and you may see these small, feathered creatures clinging to tree trunks, leaping awkwardly from branch to branch or gliding to the ground.

RECORD BREAKER

A fast-moving hunter of lizards and insects, Anchiornis is the smallest dinosaur predator yet discovered, beating out a number of other little feathered hunters, mainly from China and Mongolia, for the title.

Long tail with distinctive black-and-white banding

Shape of hind legs resembles larger theropod dinosaurs

SPOTTER STATS

Meat-eater

Length:	40cm
Weight:	250g
Speed:	Up to 30km/h
IQ:	High
Sub-order:	Theropoda
Clade:	Avialae

CRETACEOUS PERIOD

66 mya

CENOZOIC ERA

Now

ANKYLOSAURUS

An-ky-low-SAW-rus

Name means: Stiff lizard

If you hear a rumble in the jungle, chances are it's Ankylosaurus – this weighty, slow-moving dino is the tank of the Cretaceous! With mega-strong armour plates and a bone-crushing tail club, it's even tough enough to take on Tyrannosaurus.

DANGER RATING: 5

- Swinging tail club
- Bony spikes
- Head horns

Western USA, Canada

Small brain and poor eyesight make extra-strong armour essential

TRIASSIC PERIOD		JURASSIC PERIOD	
252 mya		201 mya	145 mya

MESOZOIC ERA

WHERE TO LOOK?

A camouflage jacket is a must for hiding out in the woodlands of North America, where Ankylosaurus chomps on low plants and drinks from shallow pools. Climb high up a tree (remember, this is prime Tyrannosaurus territory!) and try not to sweat – if you do Ankylosaurus will smell you from way off.

SPOTTER STATS

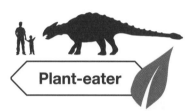

Plant-eater

Length:	7m
Weight:	4–7 tonnes
Speed:	24km/h
IQ:	Low
Sub-order:	Ornithischia
Family:	Ankylosauridae

Heavy tail club swings with great force, breaking the bones of an attacker

Low, wide body means Ankylosaurus is very hard to flip over

Rounded armour plates help to deflect predators' teeth

Massive fermentation chamber inside helps to digest huge quantities of chopped plants

CRETACEOUS PERIOD

Late Cretaceous
74–67 million years ago

66 mya

CENOZOIC ERA

Now

APATOSAURUS

Ah-pa-toe-SAW-rus

Name means: Deceptive lizard

Confusion over early fossils of this giant sauropod mean that many people know it by another name, Brontosaurus. It's one of the biggest of the big guys that roam the Late Jurassic, though it tends to keep to itself or small groups of its own kind.

DANGER RATING: 3

- Massive size
- Heavy legs
- Whip-like tail

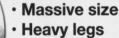

USA

WHERE TO LOOK?

Apatosaurus roams the swampy lowlands of what is now the western United States. Wear waterproof boots and be prepared to cover a wide area to keep up with it. This sauropod's large size and thick legs make it stand out from the crowd.

TRIASSIC PERIOD	JURASSIC PERIOD	
252 mya	201 mya	145 mya

MESOZOIC ERA

Late Jurassic
154–150 million years ago

SPOTTER STATS

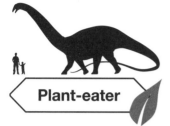

Plant-eater

Length:	23–33m
Weight:	20 tonnes
Speed:	Up to 16km/h
IQ:	Low
Sub-order:	Sauropodomorpha
Family:	Diplodocidae

Tail tapers to a narrow, whip-like tip that can be flicked or cracked at predators

Massive, deep chest with very long ribs

Huge muscles at base of tail support its extraordinary length

Wider, heavier legs than most sauropods, to support vast bulk

Single claw on each front foot, three claws on each back foot

CRETACEOUS PERIOD

66 mya

CENOZOIC ERA

Now

ARCHAEOPTERYX

Ar-kay-OP-ter-ix

Name means: Ancient feather

This little guy doesn't just look like a bird, but essentially is one. It's the link between the group of feathered dinosaurs common in the late Jurassic and the birds we're familiar with today. Yep, those fluffy little things flitting around your garden are actually dinosaurs!

DANGER RATING:

1

- Spiky little teeth
- Sharp claws
- About a third of your size, so nothing to worry about

Beak-like narrow jaws lined with small teeth

Long, separate fingers with large claws, useful for gripping branches

Germany

Runs fast on strong feet, with large second toe raised

TRIASSIC PERIOD	JURASSIC PERIOD
252 mya	201 mya

MESOZOIC ERA

145 mya

Late Jurassic
155–150 million years ago

WHERE TO LOOK?

You'll need a small boat to reach the islands where Archaeopteryx dwells, amid a warm, shallow sea. Scan the water's edge and you might spot one scurrying around on its strong legs, snapping up small prey and dead fish, occasionally leaping and gliding to catch things in mid-air.

Big feathers on wings and tail

Shorter, fluffier feathers on body and legs help keep Archaeopteryx warm

RECORD BREAKER

You're looking at the earliest bird species yet discovered. It evolved from small, predatory, feathered dinosaurs, having developed features that are typical of today's birds, such as longer wing feathers and the power of flight.

SPOTTER STATS

Meat-eater

Length:	50cm
Weight:	500g
Speed:	30km/h on ground
IQ:	High
Sub-order:	Theropoda
Clade:	Avialae

CRETACEOUS PERIOD

66 mya

CENOZOIC ERA

Now

ARGENTINOSAURUS

Ar-jen-teen-oh-SAW-rus

Name means: Lizard from Argentina

Is that the ground shaking beneath your feet? Could it be an earthquake? No, it's an approaching herd of Argentinosaurus. Among the heaviest creatures that have ever lived, these astonishingly massive sauropods rumble across the plains in groups of a dozen or more, devouring almost every bit of vegetation in their path.

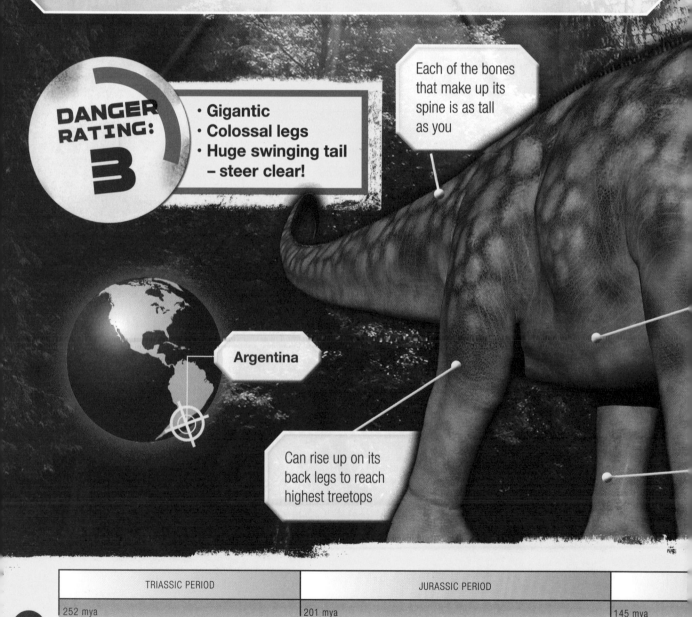

DANGER RATING: 3

- Gigantic
- Colossal legs
- Huge swinging tail – steer clear!

Each of the bones that make up its spine is as tall as you

Argentina

Can rise up on its back legs to reach highest treetops

TRIASSIC PERIOD	JURASSIC PERIOD	
252 mya	201 mya	145 mya

MESOZOIC ERA

Small head relative to size of body

Rips off vegetation using long, spoon-like teeth, then swallows it whole

WHERE TO LOOK?

Explore the open shrublands and conifer forests of central South America, looking for herds of Argentinosaurus grazing on the plains or tearing at towering trees. Stumble upon a nesting site and you might be lucky enough to witness one of the annual gatherings during which hundreds of these giants come together to lay their eggs.

Gastroliths help pound tough plant matter into a more digestible paste

SPOTTER STATS

Plant-eater

Length:	30m
Weight:	70–80 tonnes
Speed:	8km/h
IQ:	Low
Sub-order:	Sauropodomorpha
Clade:	Titanosauria

Colossal, pillar-like legs to support immense body weight

CRETACEOUS PERIOD

Late Cretaceous
97–94 million years ago

66 mya

CENOZOIC ERA

Now

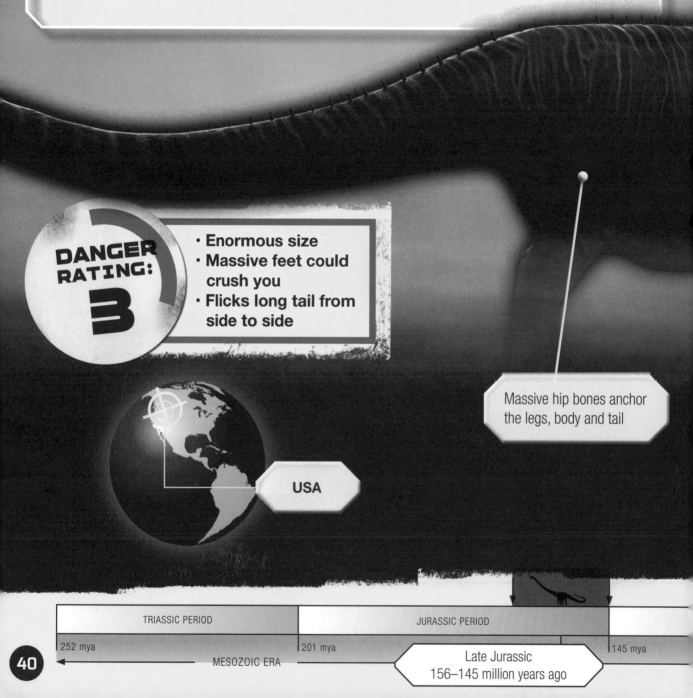

BAROSAURUS

Bah-roh-SAW-rus

Name means: Heavy lizard

With lots of giant sauropods around in the Late Jurassic, there's plenty of competition for food. Barosaurus beats out most of its rivals by a neck – a very long one. This allows it to stretch higher and further across the ground and into trees to snack on food smaller relatives can't reach.

DANGER RATING:

3

- Enormous size
- Massive feet could crush you
- Flicks long tail from side to side

Massive hip bones anchor the legs, body and tail

USA

TRIASSIC PERIOD	JURASSIC PERIOD	
252 mya	201 mya	145 mya

MESOZOIC ERA

Late Jurassic
156–145 million years ago

WHERE TO LOOK?

It's warm and humid in Jurassic North America, so dress in light clothing and carry rain gear in case of downpours. Like other sauropods of this period, Barosaurus tends to roam in herds. Watch closely and you'll see that it feeds by sweeping its head in a wide arc across low-growing plants or reaching into conifer trees.

Small, light, rectangular skull with peg-like teeth for ripping off foliage, which is swallowed whole

Exceptionally long neck, up to 10m long, provides extra reach

Neck can swing from side to side but cannot be lifted very high

Cavities in bones make neck lighter

SPOTTER STATS

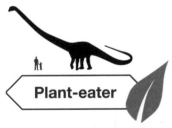

Plant-eater

Length:	27m
Weight:	20–30 tonnes
Speed:	16km/h
IQ:	Low
Sub-order:	Sauropodomorpha
Family:	Diplodocidae

CRETACEOUS PERIOD

66 mya

CENOZOIC ERA

Now

BRACHIOSAURUS

Brack-ee-oh-SAW-rus

Name means: Arm lizard

Going up! While most sauropods stretch treewards at a low angle, Brachiosaurus stands tall and straight on long front legs and with its neck erect. That way it reaches all the highest branches – and no doubt enjoys a great view!

DANGER RATING: 2

- Massive body
- Powerful front legs
- Shorter tail than other sauropods

Enormous size deters virtually all predators

USA

Short, tapering, inflexible tail to balance forward tilt of head and neck

TRIASSIC PERIOD	JURASSIC PERIOD	
252 mya	201 mya	145 mya

MESOZOIC ERA

Late Jurassic
150–145 million years ago

WHERE TO LOOK?

Clusters of big conifer trees dot the plains of western North America. These are the best places to look for Brachiosaurus, as they're where it enjoys the greatest advantage over other sauropods. Standing tall it reaches as high as a five-storey building, so it's likely to see you coming!

Long neck (up to 10m) held upright, body angled down towards tail, overall shape something like a giraffe

Larger head than most sauropods, with distinctive bulge on top housing wide nasal airways

52 long, chisel-like teeth at front of jaw, used to cut through tough plants, which are then swallowed whole

Especially tall and strong front legs allow Brachiosaurus to stand more upright than other sauropods – the upper bone alone is as long as an adult human

SPOTTER STATS

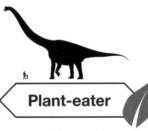

Plant-eater

Length:	23m
Weight:	35 tonnes
Speed:	10km/h
IQ:	Low
Sub-order:	Sauropodomorpha
Family:	Brachiosauridae

CITIPATI

Sit-ee-PA-tee

Name means: Lord of the funeral pyre

You've probably never seen anything like this before! With its feathers, short wings, long neck and beak, Citipati resembles some sort of huge, prehistoric emu. And although it is in fact a feathered dinosaur, it behaves in many ways like a bird.

DANGER RATING:

3

- **Powerful legs and kick**
- **Sharp claws**
- **Big and weird – might give you a fright!**

Long tail with fan-like arrangement of feathers at tip

Mongolia

Covering of short, downy feathers on body provides warmth in cold Mongolian desert

TRIASSIC PERIOD	JURASSIC PERIOD	
252 mya	201 mya	145 mya

Hollow, bony head crest, covered in tough, horn-like material

No teeth, but has bony prongs on the roof of its mouth – good for cracking open shellfish

WHERE TO LOOK?

Look for Citipati along desert lakeshores, where it often paddles in shallow water, feeding on fish and shellfish. Creep silently into neighbouring dunes and you may be lucky enough to spy one sitting on its nest just like a modern bird, its feathered arms spread across a clutch of oval eggs.

Strong, hooked claws for catching fish, grabbing small animals and digging up insects

SPOTTER STATS

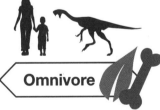

Omnivore

Length:	2.5m
Weight:	75kg
Speed:	48km/h
IQ:	High
Sub-order:	Theropoda
Family:	Oviraptoridae

CRETACEOUS PERIOD

66 mya

Late Cretaceous
84–74 million years ago

CENOZOIC ERA

Now

COAHUILACERATOPS

Coh-whee-lah-SER-ra-tops

Name means: Horn face from Coahuila (in Mexico)

The gigantic horns on this massive herbivore send a clear message to would-be predators: back off! And with its armour-like head frill and, usually, a bunch of mates in tow, Coahuilaceratops would make even the most fearsome carnivore think twice about attacking.

DANGER RATING: 5

- Spear-like horns
- Massive bulk
- May charge when threatened

Head frill also used for display and controlling body temperature

Wide, armoured frill, fringed with arrowhead-like bony lumps, protects neck

RECORD BREAKER

Coahuilaceratops has the longest and thickest horns yet discovered on any dinosaur. Strong, curved and tapering to a sharp point, each one measures more than 1m in length.

Mexico

TRIASSIC PERIOD	JURASSIC PERIOD	
252 mya	201 mya	145 mya

MESOZOIC ERA

Huge horns made of bone but covered with live tissue to provide flexibility and durability

WHERE TO LOOK?

Scan the plains for herds of these herbivores grazing on shrubs, ferns and mosses. Watch them for a while and you may see rival males using their horns to fight each other.

Short, stumpy nose horn

Hooked bone at front of upper jaw is unique to horned dinosaurs

Strong, beak-like mouth, good for ripping up plants

SPOTTER STATS

Plant-eater

Length:	7m
Weight:	5 tonnes
Speed:	25km/h
IQ:	Low
Order:	Ornithischia
Family:	Ceratopsidae

CRETACEOUS PERIOD

66 mya

Now

Late Cretaceous
72–70 million years ago

CENOZOIC ERA

COELOPHYSIS
See-LOW-fye-sis

Name means: Hollow form (a reference to its hollow bones)

They could come upon you suddenly, a pack of these agile hunters speeding through the trees and ferns, snapping up every little creature in their path. So be on the alert and if you see them, move well back, stay quiet, hold your breath – and let them pass!

Narrow snout lined with sharp, serrated teeth, ideal for catching small animals

Large, forward-facing eyes provide excellent vision, able to spot even tiny creatures from afar

DANGER RATING:
7

- Hunts in packs
- Very fast
- Sharp claws and teeth

USA

Three sharp claws on each hand for grasping prey

TRIASSIC PERIOD	JURASSIC PERIOD	
252 mya	201 mya	145 mya

Late Triassic
216–201 million years ago

MESOZOIC ERA

SPOTTER STATS

Meat-eater

Length:	3m
Weight:	25kg
Speed:	48km/h
IQ:	High
Sub-order:	Sauropodomorpha
Family:	Dicraeosauridae

Long, slender, muscular body with light bones and strong legs – built for speed and agility

Long tail assists with balance when running

Strong, broad, three-clawed feet provide stability, balance and speed

WHERE TO LOOK?

Search around the conifer forests that dot North America's arid open plains and fringe its rivers and lakes. For safety, it's best to climb a tree and watch from above. You'll see Coelophysis snacking on an array of small animals, from insects and lizards to some of the earliest (small) mammals. They'll even eat their own young and each other if they are really hungry!

CRETACEOUS PERIOD

66 mya

Now

CENOZOIC ERA

CRYOLOPHOSAURUS

Cry-oh-loaf-oh-SAW-rus

Name means: Frozen crested lizard

As Antarctica's largest predator, Cryolophosaurus already stands out from the crowd. But what makes it unique among carnivores is its forward-facing head crest. Something like a stylish rock'n'roll quiff, it has earned this creature the nickname of Elvisaurus!

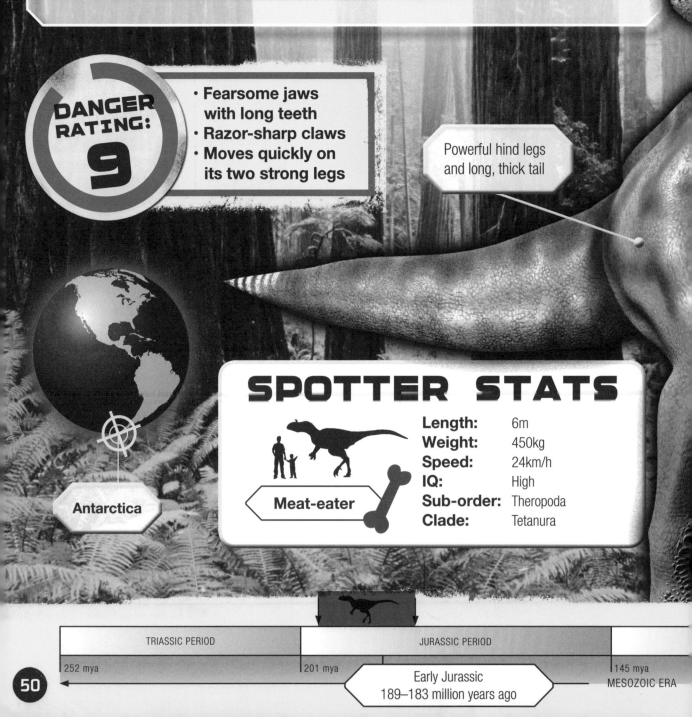

DANGER RATING:

9

- Fearsome jaws with long teeth
- Razor-sharp claws
- Moves quickly on its two strong legs

Powerful hind legs and long, thick tail

Antarctica

SPOTTER STATS

Meat-eater

Length:	6m
Weight:	450kg
Speed:	24km/h
IQ:	High
Sub-order:	Theropoda
Clade:	Tetanura

TRIASSIC PERIOD	JURASSIC PERIOD	
252 mya	201 mya	145 mya
	Early Jurassic 189–183 million years ago	MESOZOIC ERA

Distinctive grooved, fan-shaped head crest, probably used in mating or territorial displays

Small horns protect against other predators

Strong jaws with numerous sharp teeth, ideal for killing and eating small and large prey and ripping up dead animals

WHERE TO LOOK?

You'll have to wrap up warm for the cool Jurassic climate in these Antarctic realms and move cautiously through the giant conifer trees, taking cover at any sign of danger. Keep your fingers crossed that Cryolophosaurus is distracted by other, larger prey.

RECORD BREAKER

Cryolophosaurus fossils were found just 650km from what is now the South Pole. That makes this the most southerly dinosaur ever discovered.

Short arms, but with three long claws for seizing prey

CRETACEOUS PERIOD

66 mya

CENOZOIC ERA

Now

DEINOCHEIRUS

Dine-oh-KY-rus

Name means: Terrible hands

Seen from a distance, it's something like an ostrich. But as it gets close you'll realise: that would be one heck of an ostrich! Deinocheirus is a towering, slender dinosaur that can speed along on its strong legs and giant three-toed feet.

Body covered with short, hair-like feathers, which provide warmth in cool Mongolian interior

DANGER RATING: 5

- Prefers plants but partial to the odd meaty snack
- Powerful hooked claws
- Huge and very fast

Mongolia

RECORD BREAKER

With its lanky limbs and long, highly flexible neck, Deinocheirus stands tall – really tall! In fact, it's the tallest of all theropods, even looking down on the likes of Tarbosaurus, its main predator.

TRIASSIC PERIOD	JURASSIC PERIOD	
252 mya	201 mya	145 mya

MESOZOIC ERA

Massive arms, each measuring up to 2.5m in length

WHERE TO LOOK?

Explore the wetland forests of Mongolia's Nemegt Basin. Look for foliage shaking, or even the head of Deinocheirus rising above the forest canopy. It uses its height to feed on the tallest trees, which are beyond the reach of the other herbivores in this region.

SPOTTER STATS

Omnivore

Length:	12m
Weight:	6 tonnes
Speed:	40km/h
IQ:	High
Sub-order:	Theropoda
Family:	Deinocheiridae

Long back legs, standing up to 3.6m tall at the hip

Giant hands, each with three strong, hooked claws, ideal for pulling down branches

Wide, muscular feet provide strong support and rapid acceleration

Each claw at the end of the fingers is about 30cm long

CRETACEOUS PERIOD

66 mya

Now

Late Cretaceous 70–66 million years ago

CENOZOIC ERA

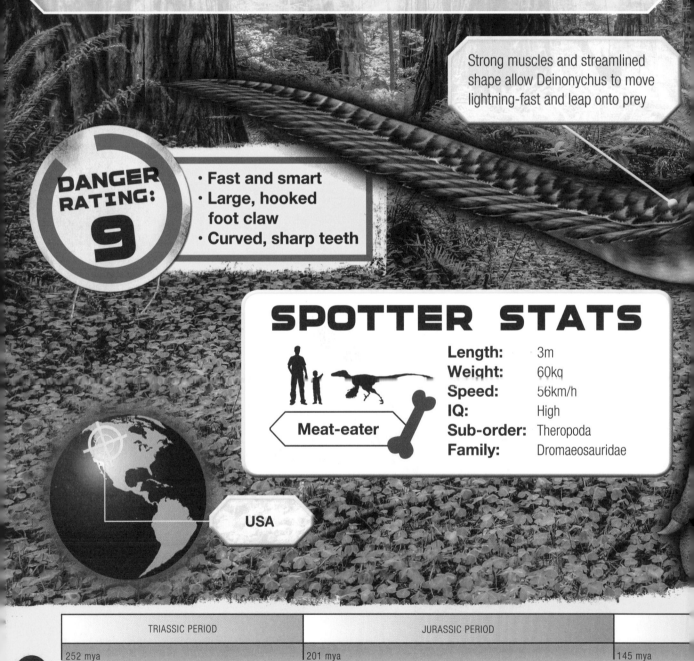

DEINONYCHUS

Dine-oh-NYE-chus

Name means: Terrible claw

About your size, slender and fringed with fluffy feathers, Deinonychus looks kind of cute. But don't be fooled. This is one of the dinosaur world's most cunning, vicious and successful hunters. Be afraid, very afraid!

Strong muscles and streamlined shape allow Deinonychus to move lightning-fast and leap onto prey

DANGER RATING:

9

- Fast and smart
- Large, hooked foot claw
- Curved, sharp teeth

SPOTTER STATS

Meat-eater

Length:	3m
Weight:	60kg
Speed:	56km/h
IQ:	High
Sub-order:	Theropoda
Family:	Dromaeosauridae

USA

TRIASSIC PERIOD	JURASSIC PERIOD	
252 mya	201 mya	145 mya

WHERE TO LOOK?

Take the utmost care when exploring the forest-cloaked hills that are home to Deinonychus, for there's no way you can outrun this predator. Find a high, secure spot, such as a cliff-top, and keep your eyes peeled for small, feathered forms flashing across clearings in pursuit of prey.

Tightly spaced, small, curved teeth, ideal for ripping into flesh and tearing up kills

Feathers fan out around arms, behind head and along tail

Curved middle claw on both feet gouges deep and then rips victim open

Long fingers tipped with razor-sharp claws, perfect for slicing flesh

CRETACEOUS PERIOD

66 mya

Now

Early Cretaceous
115–108 million years ago

CENOZOIC ERA

DIPLODOCUS

Dip-LOH-doh-cus

Name means: Double beam (a reference to the shape of its tailbones)

It's true that it's lumbering, slow and not so smart. But Diplodocus has a surprise in store for any predators that think it's a big, easy target – a long, thin but heavy tail that can strike like a whip, and at supersonic speeds.

Tiny head (60cm long) in relation to its body, with a small mouth filled with peg-like teeth designed for stripping foliage

Spiky fringe of triangular spines runs along its back – more for display than defence

DANGER RATING:

4

- **Colossal size**
- **Whip-like tail**
- **May lash out, kick or charge if threatened**

USA

Huge neck, up to 7m long; air pockets in bones make neck lighter and easier to support

TRIASSIC PERIOD	JURASSIC PERIOD	
252 mya	201 mya	145 mya

MESOZOIC ERA

Late Jurassic
150–145 million years ago

WHERE TO LOOK?

Hard to miss, herds of Diplodocus are always on the move across the well-watered plains, searching for lush pockets of Jurassic forest where they can feast on foliage. Diplodocus travels slowly and isn't aggressive, so you should be able to get close enough for a good view – but watch out for that tail!

Enormous double-beam tailbones anchor the massive weight of the tail and support rapid movement

Tough hide is covered in round, knobbly scales

Long, tapering, highly flexible tail, stretching up to 14m

RECORD BREAKER

Diplodocus flexes its tail like a whip, swiping it at attackers but also flicking it to make a deafening crack that scares off enemies and attracts mates. To make that sound, the tail has to travel at more than 1206km/h – faster than any other dinosaur's tail can move.

SPOTTER STATS

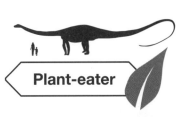

Plant-eater

Length:	32m
Weight:	30 tonnes
Speed:	16km/h
IQ:	Low
Sub-order:	Sauropodomorpha
Family:	Diplodocidae

EDMONTONIA

Ed-mon-TOE-nee-ah

Name means: From Edmonton (in Canada, where fossils were found)

This guy is ready for anything! Almost every part of Edmontonia's head, back and tail is clad with armour and studded with spikes, and its broad, powerful, low-slung body means it's never going to be a pushover, even for the biggest predators.

DANGER RATING: 5

- Heavily armoured
- Covered with spikes
- Usually placid, but can charge like a bull

Tough, knobbly skin covers head and face; bony ridges provide further protection around eyes

USA, Canada

TRIASSIC PERIOD	JURASSIC PERIOD	
252 mya	201 mya	145 mya

MESOZOIC ERA

Square plates of armour arranged across the upper back to provide protection in battles

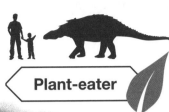

Plant-eater

Length:	6m
Weight:	3 tonnes
Speed:	24km/h
IQ:	Low
Order:	Ornithischia
Family:	Nodosauridae

Sharp spikes along sides can inflict severe injury on opponents

The largest spikes, at the front, are forked; rival males may lock these spines together when fighting

Short, muscular legs provide a rock-solid foundation

RECORD BREAKER

Edmontonia is the spikiest dinosaur of all time. Spikes of all shapes and sizes jut out from all over its body. Some scientists think they may be even longer and sharper than shown here.

WHERE TO LOOK?

Wear waterproof boots to track Edmontonia through the marshy North American Jurassic forests. You'll usually find it munching on shrubs and ferns around muddy ponds. It doesn't move much, but if it looks your way and breaks into a run, get out quick!

CRETACEOUS PERIOD

66 mya

Now

Late Cretaceous
70–66 million years ago

CENOZOIC ERA

EDMONTOSAURUS

Ed-mon-toe-SAW-rus

Name means: Lizard from Edmonton (in Canada, where fossils were found)

You've heard of a duck-billed platypus? Well this is a duckbilled dinosaur, or hadrosaur. Aside from the bill, however, ducks and Edmontosaurus have very little in common. For this humungous herbivore has hundreds of teeth and is as big as a bus.

DANGER RATING: 2

- Don't get in its way, it's big!
- Lots of teeth
- Heavy, swinging tail

Stands or walks slowly on four feet, but runs on its back legs

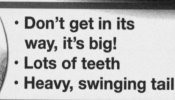

USA, Canada

RECORD BREAKER

You'd hardly know it, as it keeps them well hidden, but Edmontosaurus has the most teeth of any dinosaur. Rows and rows of little diamond-shaped gnashers line the back of its mouth – more than 1000 in all!

TRIASSIC PERIOD	JURASSIC PERIOD	
252 mya	201 mya	145 mya

MESOZOIC ERA

WHERE TO LOOK?

Don your wet-weather gear and head for central North America's conifer-fringed swamps. Look for groups of Edmontosaurus (they like to stick together) ripping at shrubs and ferns. Try not to startle them or they could stampede.

Large eyes and sensitive hearing provide early warning of approaching predators

Teeth arranged in rows; when one row wears out, another replaces it

Jaw moves back and forth horizontally, grinding plant matter between teeth

Broad beak made of same horn-like material as beaks of today's birds and turtles

SPOTTER STATS

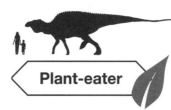

Plant-eater

Length:	9m
Weight:	4 tonnes
Speed:	40km/h
IQ:	Low
Order:	Ornithischia
Family:	Hadrosauridae

CRETACEOUS PERIOD

66 mya

Now

Late Cretaceous
70–66 million years ago

CENOZOIC ERA

EORAPTOR

EE-oh-rap-tor

Name means: Dawn plunderer

Eoraptor is only as big as a medium-sized, skinny dog, but probably more vicious and dangerous than any dog you have ever met. Take a look at those teeth and those curved, lethally sharp claws. No way are you going to pat that!

DANGER RATING:

6

- **Small but fierce**
- **Razor-sharp teeth**
- **Large front claws**

Curved, serrated front teeth for ripping up prey; smaller, leaf-shaped back teeth for grinding

Argentina

WHERE TO LOOK?

Pack your waterproof jacket in case you happen upon a rainy spell in the increasingly humid Late Triassic environment. Look for Eoraptors scurrying through the undergrowth, and give them a wide berth. They'll be on the alert for the giant, crocodile-like reptiles called archosaurs. You should be too!

TRIASSIC PERIOD		JURASSIC PERIOD	
252 mya		201 mya	145 mya

Late Triassic
231–228 million years ago

MESOZOIC ERA

SPOTTER STATS

Omnivore

Length:	1m
Weight:	10kg
Speed:	30km/h
IQ:	Medium
Order:	Saurischia
Sub-order:	Theropoda

Light, muscular, agile body makes it highly manoeuvrable

Scavenges on dead animals and some plant matter, as well as hunting prey

Long tail used to assist balance when running

Short arms and large hands with three long fingers tipped with hooked claws for grasping prey

Speeds along on strong back legs

CRETACEOUS PERIOD

66 mya

Now

CENOZOIC ERA

EUOPLOCEPHALUS

You-OH-plo-kef-ah-luss

Name means: Well-armed head

Like a medieval knight, Euoplocephalus is cloaked with armour and wields a deadly weapon – in this case, a massive hammer-like club at the end of its tail. One swing of that will make any predator think twice about attacking!

Wide, heavy, hammer-like tail club – great for smashing the leg bones of predators

DANGER RATING: 5

- **Massive club at end of tail**
- **Head and shoulder spikes**
- **Heavy enough to flatten you**

Fermentation chamber in stomach helps digest tough plants – and also produces lots of smelly gases!

USA, Canada

TRIASSIC PERIOD	JURASSIC PERIOD	
252 mya	201 mya	145 mya

MESOZOIC ERA

Bony plates, ridges and spikes cover head, neck and back, providing protection against teeth and claws

SPOTTER STATS

Plant-eater

Length:	6m
Weight:	2 tonnes
Speed:	24km/h
IQ:	Low
Order:	Ornithischia
Family:	Ankylosauridae

Stiff, shutter-like, bony plates can slide down to shield eyes

Horny beak helps rip up tough plant matter

Wide body and low centre of gravity make it difficult for attackers to turn Euoplocephalus over

WHERE TO LOOK?

Search for small groups of these tank-like creatures roaming the plains, browsing on bushes and shrubs and pulling up roots from the soil. Should a predator approach, Euoplocephalus will stand its ground and start swinging its tail until its foe backs off, often battered and bruised.

CRETACEOUS PERIOD

66 mya

Now

Late Cretaceous
76–66 million years ago

CENOZOIC ERA

FRUITADENS
FROOT-ah-dens

Name means: Fruita tooth (after the town of Fruita, USA, where fossils were found)

You'll have to be sharp-eyed to spot this one! No bigger than the average cat today, tiny Fruitadens tears around on its strong back legs, keeping a low profile as it gathers leaves and fruit from trees and snaps up lizards and insects.

Teeth at back of jaw chew fruit and grind up tough plant matter

DANGER RATING: 2

- Sharp claws
- Small, pointy fangs
- Could give you a nip!

Hard beak with short, sharp fangs on lower jaw, used to bite food, fight attackers and make scary faces at rivals and predators

USA

Sharp, hooked claws on hands, useful for pulling down branches and spearing food

TRIASSIC PERIOD	JURASSIC PERIOD	
252 mya	201 mya	145 mya

MESOZOIC ERA

Late Jurassic 153–145 million years ago

WHERE TO LOOK?

Fruitadens likes areas with dense, low foliage that provide extensive cover. Needing only a modest amount of food to fuel its little body, it confines its outings to a small area, usually around fruit trees.

RECORD BREAKER

Fruitadens isn't just small, it's the smallest plant-eating dinosaur of all time. It's a dangerous world for these titchiest of guys, so, when not hunting, they hide out in dense undergrowth.

Strong back legs provide speed and rapid acceleration – vital in times of danger

Long, strong, flexible tail improves balance when running on two legs

SPOTTER STATS

Omnivore

Length:	70cm
Weight:	About 800g
Speed:	40km/h
IQ:	Not known
Order:	Ornithischia
Family:	Heterodontosauridae

GALLIMIMUS

Gal-leh-MY-mus

Name means: Chicken mimic

When danger nears and things are looking threatening, often the best idea is just to run for it. And Gallimimus is certainly good at that. One of the swiftest of dinosaurs, it can clock up an impressive top speed of around 45km/h – pretty nippy for a big guy!

DANGER RATING:

2

- Sharp claws
- Huge body
- Might run you over if you get in its way

Long, heavy tail helps maintain balance when turning at top speed

SPOTTER STATS

Omnivore

Length:	6m
Weight:	450kg
Speed:	45km/h
IQ:	High
Sub-order:	Theropoda
Family:	Ornithomimidae

Mongolia

TRIASSIC PERIOD	JURASSIC PERIOD	
252 mya	201 mya	145 mya

MESOZOIC ERA

Eyes at side of head allow Gallimimus to keep watch in all directions

Large toothless beak with shovel-like lower jaw for scooping up food

RECORD BREAKER

Gallimimus is the second fastest dinosaur of all time, after its close relative Struthiomimus. Both are members of the Ornithomimidae – the 'bird mimics' – and resemble ostriches, the fastest-running birds today.

Long neck and bird-like head

Short arms and small hands, with three sharp claws for scraping at ground to get at insects and worms

WHERE TO LOOK?

Gallimimus roams the humid forests and plains of Mongolia's Nemegt region, where it often wades in streams and along the edges of lakes, scooping up plant matter and small creatures. Wear your wellingtons to search these waterways, but stay alert for fearsome predators such as Tarbosaurus – unlike Gallimimus, you might not be able to outrun them!

Speeds along thanks to its big, powerful legs and strong, broad feet

CRETACEOUS PERIOD

66 mya

Now

Late Cretaceous
70–66 million years ago

CENOZOIC ERA

GIGANOTOSAURUS

Jig-ah-no-toh-SAW-rus

Name means: Giant southern lizard

This guy is South America's ultimate killing machine. Even bigger than Tyrannosaurus Rex, it can bulldoze prey to the ground with its colossal body before ripping it to pieces with its terrifying, dagger-like teeth. Steer clear!

Bony lumps and ridges protect the skull and eyes

DANGER RATING: 10

- **Even bigger than T Rex**
- **Large head and massive jaws**
- **Long, sharp teeth**

Teeth measuring up to 20cm have jagged edges like steak knives, for slicing through flesh

Argentina

Strong neck to support huge head – the skull is longer than an adult human is tall

TRIASSIC PERIOD	JURASSIC PERIOD	
252 mya	201 mya	145 mya

MESOZOIC ERA

SPOTTER STATS

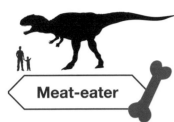

Meat-eater

Length:	12.5m
Weight:	8 tonnes
Speed:	30km/h
IQ:	Medium
Sub-order:	Theropoda
Family:	Carcharodontosauridae

Arms are short and fairly weak but have long, sharp claws for grasping prey

WHERE TO LOOK?

Be very, very careful as you search the South American shrublands and conifer forests. Giganotosaurus likes to surprise its prey by bursting out of thick stands of trees, and it sometimes hunts in packs to bring down even the biggest sauropods. With luck, it will think you're too small a snack to be worth chasing!

CRETACEOUS PERIOD

66 mya

Now

Early to Late Cretaceous
100–97 million years ago

CENOZOIC ERA

HERRERASAURUS

Er-air-uh-SAW-rus

Name means: Herrera's lizard (after the rancher who found the first fossil)

Among the first dinosaurs of the South American Triassic, Herrerasaurus is top dog. For while the region's other dinosaurs are all still fairly titchy, this species has filled out and bulked up to become one big, scary predator!

DANGER RATING: 7

- Large, serrated teeth
- Long, sharp claws
- Fast-moving

Argentina

Muscular body, with strong legs providing speed and acceleration

TRIASSIC PERIOD		JURASSIC PERIOD	
252 mya		201 mya	145 mya

Late Triassic
235–230 million years ago

MESOZOIC ERA

Big and strong enough to bring down animals much larger than itself

WHERE TO LOOK?

Head for South America's Triassic conifer forests. Tread carefully though, as Herrerasaurus will be prowling through the ferns in search of prey. Even more of a worry are giant crocodile-like reptiles called crurotarsans, which will easily devour a Herrerasaurus – or you! – given a half a chance.

Massive head with long snout and powerful jaws

About 80 curved, serrated teeth, designed for slashing at prey and ripping up flesh

Three long fingers with sharp, curved claws for slashing and pinning prey

SPOTTER STATS

Meat-eater

Length:	4m
Weight:	200kg
Speed:	48km/h
IQ:	Medium
Sub-order:	Theropoda
Family:	Herrerasauridae

HYPSELOSAURUS

Hip-sell-oh-SAW-rus

Name means: Highest lizard

Close to the end of the age of the dinosaurs, humungous sauropods, known as titanosaurs, rumble around the plains and forests of western Europe. Among them is Hypselosaurus, as long and high as a double-decker bus.

DANGER RATING: 3

- Giant body
- Coiling, whip-like tail
- Strong legs can deliver a fierce kick

RECORD BREAKER

The eggs of Hypselosaurus are the largest dinosaur eggs ever discovered. Each one is the equivalent in size of 73 chicken eggs. Amazingly, these eggs are dwarfed by those of an extinct bird from Madagascar, the elephant bird, whose eggs were four times as big!

Long, tapering tail balances long neck

Heavy, robust legs to support massive weight of body

France

Prominent claws, used to dig pit for eggs and then cover with sand

TRIASSIC PERIOD	JURASSIC PERIOD	
252 mya	201 mya	145 mya

MESOZOIC ERA

Ridge of bony, triangular spines running entire length of body

Thick, knobbly hide provides protection from predators

Hypselosaurus is likely to be spotted moving across the plains in herds or browsing on trees and shrubs. Get lucky and you might see it laying its huge eggs – or even witness a baby Hypselosaurus breaking out of its shell.

SPOTTER STATS

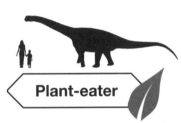

Plant-eater

Length:	15m
Weight:	7 tonnes
Speed:	16km/h
IQ:	Low
Sub-order:	Sauropodomorpha
Family:	Titanosauridae

Large, round eggs laid in lines or rough circles on open ground then buried

CRETACEOUS PERIOD

66 mya

Now

Late Cretaceous
70–66 million years ago

CENOZOIC ERA

IGUANODON

Ig-WAN-oh-don

Name means: Iguana tooth

It might look placid, and it is a plant-eater, but take heed, as Iguanodon has a deadly weapon: a huge cone-shaped spike on each hand. So approach cautiously. You don't want a big thumbs-up from this guy!

DANGER RATING:
4

- Huge body
- Strong legs – can give a fierce kick
- Dangerous thumb spikes

Toothless beak at front of jaw, but over 100 teeth at back of mouth for chewing plants

RECORD BREAKER

Iguanodon was the first plant-eating dinosaur to be identified by scientists. Initially its fossils confused them and they thought its thumb was a nose horn!

North-western Europe

Long, bendable fifth finger can be used to grab branches

TRIASSIC PERIOD	JURASSIC PERIOD	
252 mya	201 mya	
MESOZOIC ERA		Early Cretaceous 142–136 million years ago

SPOTTER STATS

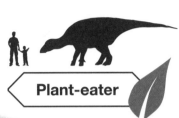

Plant-eater

Length:	8m
Weight:	3 tonnes
Speed:	20km/h
IQ:	Low
Order:	Ornithischia
Family:	Iguanodontidae

Broad body and tail, horse-like head

Walks on all four legs but can rise on its back legs to reach high branches

Huge spiked thumbs, useful for defending against predators

WHERE TO LOOK?

Iguanodons feed on medium-sized trees and flowering shrubs such as magnolias, so scan the forest edges. As long as you keep your distance, they are unlikely to take much notice of you. Watch out though for predators of Iguanodon, including toothy carnivores such as Neovenator and Baryonyx.

CRETACEOUS PERIOD

66 mya

Now

CENOZOIC ERA

LEAELLYNASAURA
Lee-ellin-ah-SAW-ra

Name means: Leaellyn's lizard (after the daughter of its discoverers)

Sometimes it pays to be small and bug-eyed. Leaellynasaura lives in the chilly forests of Early Cretaceous Australia, where it's pitch dark for three months of the year. Its large eyes help it see in low light, while its small size makes it hard for poor-sighted predators to spot.

Tail may be wrapped around body to keep warm in winter

Long tail assists balance when on the move and could be used for signalling

DANGER RATING:

1

- Hard beak but no sharp teeth
- Sharp claws could scratch
- Furry tail might tickle

RECORD BREAKER

Leaellynasaura holds the record for the longest tail, compared to the rest of its body, of any ornithischian dinosaur. Furry and flexible, its tail is three times the size of its head, neck and body combined.

South-eastern Australia

TRIASSIC PERIOD	JURASSIC PERIOD	
252 mya	201 mya	

MESOZOIC ERA

Early Cretaceous
125–120 million years ago

SPOTTER STATS

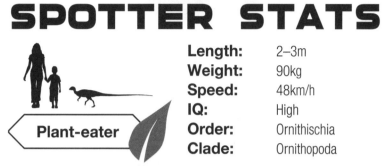

Plant-eater

Length:	2–3m
Weight:	90kg
Speed:	48km/h
IQ:	High
Order:	Ornithischia
Clade:	Ornithopoda

WHERE TO LOOK?

These southern forests are freezing in winter, when Leaellynasaura hibernates, so go at another time of year and, even in summer, wrap up well. Look for Leaellynasaura around dawn or dusk, when it tends to be most active, scurrying around in groups, usually with one or two individuals keeping watch for danger.

Large eyes help it see and find food in the dark

Large feet with long claws, ideal for digging burrows

Strong legs and light body make Leaellynasaura a fast mover

CRETACEOUS PERIOD

66 mya

Now

CENOZOIC ERA

LIOPLEURODON

Lye-oh-PLOO-roh-don

Name means: Smooth-sided teeth

As massive as a modern-day great white shark and with jaws as long as you, Liopleurodon is one of the most terrifying sea predators of the Jurassic, or any other time. The fact that it's a pliosaur – a marine reptile – rather than a dinosaur doesn't make it any less scary!

Jaws measure up to 1.5m in length

DANGER RATING: 8

- Big
- Sharp eyes
- Huge jaw with dagger-like teeth

Fearsomely strong jaws and large, curved teeth – up to 30cm long – result in a bone-crushing, flesh-ripping bite

Europe

TRIASSIC PERIOD		JURASSIC PERIOD	
252 mya	201 mya		145 mya

MESOZOIC ERA

Mid to Late Jurassic
165–145 million years ago

WHERE TO LOOK?

Whatever you do, stay out of the water! Climb a high headland overlooking the sea and you might spy Liopleurodon surging silently out of the deep to clamp its jaws onto an unwary sea creature. Or scan the shore and you could see it launching itself up the beach to snatch a paddling dinosaur.

Excellent eyesight and sharp sense of smell help locate prey in often-murky conditions

Powerful muscles help propel streamlined body through the water

Huge paddles provide brief bursts of acceleration

SPOTTER STATS

Meat-eater

Length:	5–7m
Weight:	6 tonnes
Speed:	7km/h
IQ:	Medium
Order:	Plesiosauria
Family:	Pliosauridae

CRETACEOUS PERIOD		
	66 mya	Now

CENOZOIC ERA

LORICATOSAURUS

Lor-ee-cat-oh-SAW-rus

Name means: Armoured lizard

With one swift swish of its thorny tail, Loricatosaurus can pierce a pesky predator – or impale any other unwary passerby. So give this lumbering herbivore a wide berth and admire its array of plates and spikes from afar.

DANGER RATING: 5

- **Lethally sharp spikes**
- **Heavy, swinging tail**
- **Large bulk**

Spikes run down the tail, with the largest ones at the end

This kind of tail is sometimes called a thagomizer, a name made up by US cartoonist Gary Larson

Southern Britain

Heavy body and short legs, designed for slow walking rather than running

TRIASSIC PERIOD	JURASSIC PERIOD	
252 mya	201 mya	145 mya

MESOZOIC ERA

Mid Jurassic
164–160 million years ago

SPOTTER STATS

Plant-eater

Length:	6m
Weight:	2 tonnes
Speed:	Up to 16km/h
IQ:	Low
Order:	Ornithischia
Family:	Stegosauridae

Plates and spikes covered in a tough, horny sheath that grows steadily

WHERE TO LOOK?

Scour the forests that fringe the shallow seas of Jurassic southern Britain, where Loricatosaurus grazes on conifer leaves, ferns and mosses. Relying on its spikes and plates for defence, it's not easily scared off, so you should be able to get near enough and have plenty of time to study it closely.

Large fin-shaped plates running along neck and upper back provide protection and are used in mating displays

CRETACEOUS PERIOD

66 mya

CENOZOIC ERA

Now

MEGALOSAURUS

Meg-ah-lo-SAW-rus

Name means: Giant lizard

This fearsome hunter's big bite is backed up by its hugely powerful grip. Once those strong arms and hooked claws get a hold, they rarely let go. So keep this one at much more than arm's length!

Massive head and long jaws create a powerful bite

DANGER RATING: 8

- **Big jaws lined with sharp teeth**
- **Sharp claws**
- **Fast mover**

Large, serrated, dagger-like teeth for ripping through flesh

England

Broad, powerful feet with three forward-facing claws

TRIASSIC PERIOD	JURASSIC PERIOD	
252 mya	201 mya	145 mya

MESOZOIC ERA

Mid Jurassic
167–163 million years ago

RECORD BREAKER

Megalosaurus was the very first dinosaur to be recognised by scientists, in 1824. When its fossilised bones were first found, people thought it walked on all fours like a modern lizard.

Moves on two legs with tail held high and body leaning forwards

SPOTTER STATS

Meat-eater

Length:	6m
Weight:	700kg
Speed:	48km/h
IQ:	High
Sub-order:	Theropoda
Family:	Megalosauridae

Strong arms with three long, hooked claws for pinning prey

WHERE TO LOOK?

Rain gear is required in the damp forests of Jurassic England. Megalosaurus prowls through the trees and undergrowth, stalking prey including large plant-eaters such as stegosaurs and the sauropods. Move carefully, and be ready to scurry up a tree at the slightest sign of danger.

CRETACEOUS PERIOD

66 mya | Now

CENOZOIC ERA

MICRORAPTOR

My-crow-RAP-tor

Name means: Small one who seizes

Feathers are flying in Cretaceous China, where lots of little dinosaurs are taking to the air. Among these flying dinos, perhaps the most spectacular is Microraptor. It not only has feathers on its arms but also on its legs and tail. It's a bit like a prehistoric, feathery biplane!

Fan-shaped arrangement of feathers at end of tail keeps body stable in flight

DANGER RATING:
1

- Hooked claws
- Small teeth
- No bigger than a cat

China

Hooked claw on second toe, useful for climbing, skewering larger prey and digging insects and other small creatures out of the ground and trees

TRIASSIC PERIOD	JURASSIC PERIOD	
252 mya	201 mya	
MESOZOIC ERA		Early Cretaceous 125–120 million years ago

Especially long feathers on arms and legs form two sets of wings

WHERE TO LOOK?

Seek out Microraptor in the forests of northeastern China. Few feathered dinosaurs can fly far and, despite its showy plumes, it's no exception. Watch carefully and you'll see that it uses its hooked claws to climb trees then simply glides down to snatch small prey.

Beak-shaped jaw with small teeth for chomping food

Covering of feathers keeps body warm

Feathers on legs assist with gliding and steering, but make Microraptor a clumsy runner

SPOTTER STATS

Meat-eater

Length:	70cm
Weight:	600g
Speed:	40km/h
IQ:	High
Sub-order:	Theropoda
Family:	Dromaeosauridae

CRETACEOUS PERIOD

66 mya

Now

CENOZOIC ERA

MUTTABURRASAURUS

Mutt-ah-burr-ah-SAW-rus

Name means: Lizard from Muttaburra (town in Australia where fossils were found)

You'll almost certainly hear this one coming. A big, burly plant-eater, Muttaburrasaurus thunders around in herds. It uses the prominent bony bulge on its snout to make loud honking noises to its companions. Toot, toot!

DANGER RATING:

3

- Large, powerful, heavy body
- Strong jaw
- Plenty of teeth

Wide body with thick tail and long neck

Walks on four legs but can rear up on back legs to reach high plants

Australia

TRIASSIC PERIOD	JURASSIC PERIOD	
252 mya	201 mya	145 mya

MESOZOIC ERA

Large, hollow, bony bulge at front of snout – sound echoing in this chamber creates especially loud calls

Strong jaw with row of sharp teeth for slicing through tough vegetation

WHERE TO LOOK?

Early Cretaceous Australia enjoys a balmy climate, so you can pack light. Search the forests that fringe the inland Eromanga Sea, which covers much of this region, and you'll find groups of Muttaburrasaurus shredding ferns and palm-like cycads or reaching up to yank leaves and edible seed cones off taller conifer trees.

SPOTTER STATS

Plant-eater

Length:	8m
Weight:	3 tonnes
Speed:	20km/h
IQ:	Medium
Sub-order:	Iguanodontia
Family:	Rhabdodontidae

CRETACEOUS PERIOD

66 mya

Now

CENOZOIC ERA

Early Cretaceous
112–100 million years ago

NIGERSAURUS

Nee-jehr-SAW-rus

Name means: Lizard from Niger (in West Africa)

Stumble across this in the swamps and you might get quite a fright. For this is certainly one of the strangest looking dinosaurs, with a mouth much wider than the rest of its head. Fortunately, it's a plant-eater and, while it has hundreds of teeth, it also has a very weak bite.

Eyes located at side of skull, providing a wide view of surroundings

DANGER RATING: 2

- **Slow-moving**
- **Strong head but weak bite**
- **Whip-like tail**

Jaw lined with two rows of about 60 teeth, behind which are rows of replacements – up to 500 teeth in all!

West Africa

TRIASSIC PERIOD		JURASSIC PERIOD	
252 mya		201 mya	145 mya

MESOZOIC ERA

Shorter neck than most sauropods – shaped for bending downwards rather than reaching up

Whip-like tail can be used to whack attackers

WHERE TO LOOK?

You should spot Nigersaurus from a distance, as it likes to graze in open areas of the West African floodplains, feeding on ferns and shrubs. Riverbanks are its favourite areas. Observe carefully and you'll see it moving its wide mouth forwards slowly, mowing down plants as it goes.

Body like other sauropods, with thick legs, strong shoulders, long tail

Cavities in bones make head and neck light, allowing Nigersaurus to quickly raise its head to check for danger

SPOTTER STATS

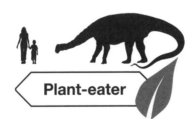

Plant-eater

Length:	9m
Weight:	2 tonnes
Speed:	16km/h
IQ:	Low
Sub-order:	Sauropodomorpha
Family:	Rebbachisauridae

CRETACEOUS PERIOD

66 mya

Now

Early Cretaceous 119–99 million years ago

CENOZOIC ERA

NYCTOSAURUS

Nik-tow-SAW-rus

Name means: Night lizard or bat lizard

With their long, pointed beaks and wide wings, the flying reptiles known as pterosaurs are already pretty bizarre. But Nyctosaurus outdoes them all with its extraordinary head crest. Four times the size of its skull, it's something like the mast on a sailboat – and may work in a similar way.

DANGER RATING:

1

- Sharp beak
- Antler-like crest
- Small and harmless – just don't get in its way!

Enormous Y-shaped crest made of bone – up to 55cm tall – used in displays to attract mates and possibly helps with steering in flight

USA

Sharp, pointed jaws, ideal for spearing prey and picking up small creatures

Small legs and feet make perching difficult and huge wings and crest make it hard to walk far – so Nyctosaurus spends most of its time in the air!

TRIASSIC PERIOD	JURASSIC PERIOD	
252 mya	201 mya	145 mya

MESOZOIC ERA

RECORD BREAKER

Compared to its body size, Nyctosaurus has by far the tallest head crest of any creature of the age of the dinosaurs. And it's the only pterosaur with an antler-like crest – all other pterosaur crests are flattened triangular or oblong shapes.

WHERE TO LOOK?

Head for the shore of the Western Interior Seaway, which covers central North America in the late Cretaceous and turn your eyes to the skies. Nyctosaurus soars over the open ocean, swooping down to snatch fish from the surface of the sea, and occasionally landing on the shore to grab shellfish, insects and worms.

Long, broad wings with a span of 2m – like those of a modern eagle – allow Nyctosaurus to fly and soar for long distances

Short body relative to wings and crest – light and easily carried aloft by the wings

SPOTTER STATS

Meat-eater

Length:	40cm body, 2m wingspan
Weight:	2.6kg
Speed:	30km/h
IQ:	High
Order:	Pterosauria
Family:	Nyctosauridae

CRETACEOUS PERIOD

66 mya

Now

Late Cretaceous
85–84 million years ago

CENOZOIC ERA

OMEISAURUS

Oh-may-SAW-rus

Name means: Lizard of Omei (the sacred mountain, Omeishan or Mt Emei, in China)

It's a wonder that this dinosaur manages to stay upright! With a neck twice the length of its body, you'd think it would just topple over. But, thanks to light bones and strong muscles, it can not only stand tall but also stretch high, far and wide to reach a vast range of plants.

DANGER RATING: 3

- Gigantic
- Massive, heavy legs
- Placid and slow-moving

Exceptionally long neck can reach high treetops and far into undergrowth

Short, rounded body, stocky legs and wide feet provide solid foundations

Short tail compared to most sauropods, but strong enough to thump attackers!

China

TRIASSIC PERIOD	JURASSIC PERIOD	
252 mya	201 mya	145 mya

MESOZOIC ERA

Mid to Late Jurassic
164–160 million years ago

Long, thin neck is also a weak point as it is easy for predators to grasp

Oval-shaped head not much wider than the neck

Strong teeth for tearing tough vegetation – eats up to 1 tonne of plants a day

RECORD BREAKER

Omeisaurus's neck is as long as two cars. Though other dinosaurs had longer necks, Omeisaurus has the longest neck of all compared to the size of its body.

WHERE TO LOOK?

Put on your wet-weather gear and explore the damp Jurassic plains and forests of central China. You'll likely see Omeisaurus's head before its body – popping up above the canopy or swooping down into a clearing to tear up ferns and cycads. A herd of these giants feeding together is a dramatic sight!

SPOTTER STATS

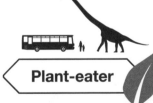

Plant-eater

Length:	18m
Weight:	8.5 tonnes
Speed:	16km/h
IQ:	Low
Sub-order:	Sauropodomorpha
Family:	Mamenchisauridae

CRETACEOUS PERIOD

66 mya

Now

CENOZOIC ERA

OPHTHALMOSAURUS

Off-thal-mow-SAW-rus

Name means: Eye lizard

In the murky underwater world of the Jurassic oceans, this dolphin-shaped ichthyosaur, a marine reptile, is one of the most successful hunters. And that's thanks mainly to a pair of powerful, outsized peepers!

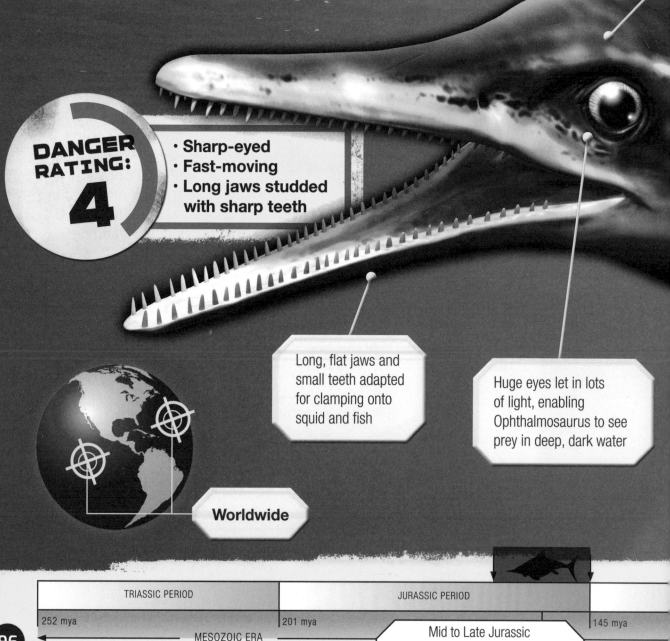

DANGER RATING: 4

- Sharp-eyed
- Fast-moving
- Long jaws studded with sharp teeth

Long, flat jaws and small teeth adapted for clamping onto squid and fish

Huge eyes let in lots of light, enabling Ophthalmosaurus to see prey in deep, dark water

Worldwide

TRIASSIC PERIOD	JURASSIC PERIOD	
252 mya	201 mya	145 mya

MESOZOIC ERA

Mid to Late Jurassic
165–145 million years ago

Ring of bone around eye and fluid inside maintain eye shape even under intense pressure of deep sea

Meat-eater

Length:	4m
Weight:	1 tonne
Speed:	30km/h
IQ:	Medium
Order:	Ichthyosauria
Family:	Ophthalmosauridae

Broad, muscular, stream-lined body with fins and paddles for steering

Powerful tail propels it through water at speed

RECORD BREAKER

Compared to the size of its body, Ophthalmosaurus has the largest eyes of any creature. About 23cm in diameter, each one is the size of a melon.

WHERE TO LOOK?

Ophthalmosaurus spends much of its time in deep water, so it's hard to spot, but it has to come up for air at least every 20 minutes or so. Look for it surfacing or speeding upwards to snap small prey. Diving down to meet it is not recommended!

CRETACEOUS PERIOD

66 mya

Now

CENOZOIC ERA

PACHYCEPHALOSAURUS

Pack-ee-SEFF-al-oh-SAW-rus

Name means: Thick-headed lizard

This one's a real head case! A stocky two-legged omnivore, Pachycephalosaurus has a bulging, dome-shaped skull surrounded by bumps and spikes. It's an arrangement that attracts female attention and is also handy for butting rivals.

Long, stiff tail assists balance when running fast

SPOTTER STATS

Omnivore

Length:	5m
Weight:	500kg
Speed:	32km/h
IQ:	Medium
Order:	Ornithischia
Family:	Pachycephalosauridae

DANGER RATING: 3

- Fast-moving
- Large clawed feet
- Head spikes

USA, Canada

Walks on two legs supported by strong, broad feet with three large, forward-facing claws

TRIASSIC PERIOD	JURASSIC PERIOD	
252 mya	201 mya	145 mya

MESOZOIC ERA

Prominent spikes and bumps on head help attract mates

RECORD BREAKER

Pachycephalosaurus has the hardest head of any dinosaur. The roof of its skull is 25cm thick. In comparison, the top of your skull is less than 1cm thick.

Thick, domed skull offers protection and can be used to butt rivals' flanks

WHERE TO LOOK?

Pachycephalosaurus trots around the plains and woodlands of Late Cretaceous North America, nibbling on soft plants and scooping up seeds and insects (fortunately the only meat it eats). Watch for a while and you might spy rival males ramming each other with their strong skulls – you could say they're often at loggerheads!

Short arms with small hands and five fingers, useful for grasping plants

CRETACEOUS PERIOD

Late Cretaceous
70–66 million years ago

66 mya

CENOZOIC ERA

Now

PARASAUROLOPHUS

Par-ah-saw-ra-LOW-fuss

Name means: Near crested lizard

What on earth is that noise like a foghorn, booming across the plains? Most likely it's the call of this unmistakeable herbivore. Its extraordinary long, curved crest contains hollow airways that allow it to make deep, honking sounds to communicate with others of its kind.

DANGER RATING: 3

- Massive
- Runs fast in large herds, so could knock you over
- Crest is not a danger

Rounded, toothless beak for pulling and ripping roots, leaves and twigs

USA, Canada

Rows of teeth in cheeks for chewing food, which are replaced regularly

TRIASSIC PERIOD	JURASSIC PERIOD	
252 mya	201 mya	145 mya

MESOZOIC ERA

WHERE TO LOOK?

Listen for the calls or look across the plains for clouds of dust, raised as these big plant-eaters thunder around in herds at high speed, searching for food. Gradually, you'll learn to distinguish its calls from those of other crested relatives like Lambeosaurus. You might even work out what they are saying!

Curved, bony crest is up to 1m long and contains long, hollow tubes

Crest used for making sounds and also for attracting mates

SPOTTER STATS

Plant-eater

Length:	7.5m
Weight:	2.6 tonnes
Speed:	40km/h
IQ:	Medium
Order:	Ornithischia
Family:	Hadrosauridae

Large body and short, thick, tapering tail

CRETACEOUS PERIOD

66 mya

Now

Late Cretaceous
76–73 million years ago

CENOZOIC ERA

PELECANIMIMUS

Pel-eh-can-ee-MIME-us

Name means: Pelican mimic

Here's a puzzle. The dinosaurs known as the ornithomimosaurs, or ostrich dinosaurs, are notable for having no teeth, just a bird-like beak. All of them, that is, except Pelecanimimus, which has more than 200 teeth. Maybe you can find out why!

Soft crest on head, possibly used to attract mates

DANGER RATING:

3

- Sharp claws
- Lots of teeth
- Unlikely to pick on something as big as you

Large eyes help spot small prey while on the move

Spain

Bag-like skin sac in throat – like that of a modern pelican – used to store food

TRIASSIC PERIOD	JURASSIC PERIOD	
252 mya	201 mya	

MESOZOIC ERA

Early Cretaceous
144–137 million years ago

SPOTTER STATS

Omnivore

Length:	2.5m
Weight:	30kg
Speed:	48km/h
IQ:	High
Sub-order:	Theropoda
Clade:	Ornithomimosauria

About 70 small teeth in upper jaw; those at the front are D-shaped, those at the back are peg-like

Long, narrow snout with around 150 tiny teeth in lower jaw

WHERE TO LOOK?

Patrol southwestern Europe's forest edges and shorelines. Pelecanimimus speeds around snapping up lizards and insects and nibbling plants. It particularly likes to wade in shallow water, reaching down to clamp its jaws onto small, slippery sea creatures.

RECORD BREAKER

Pelecanimimus not only has more teeth than other ornithomimosaurs, it has more teeth than any other dinosaur predator – up to 220 small, pointy pearly whites!

CRETACEOUS PERIOD

66 mya

CENOZOIC ERA

Now

PENTACERATOPS

Pen-ta-SER-ra-tops

Name means: Five-horned face

Now here's a dino with a lot of front! Its massive skull, horns and giant frill combine to give Pentaceratops a truly gargantuan head. The frill not only helps scare off predators but may also help it stay cool in hot weather. Nifty, eh?

DANGER RATING:

4

- **Big and powerful**
- **Huge horns**
- **Strong jaws – but still a herbivore**

Frill formed by frame of bones, extending out from the skull, covered with skin and edged with bony lumps

Large horns used to fight off predators, attract mates and duel with rivals

USA

SPOTTER STATS

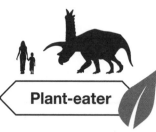

Plant-eater

Length:	7m
Weight:	5 tonnes
Speed:	32km/h
IQ:	Medium
Order:	Ornithischia
Family:	Ceratopsidae

TRIASSIC PERIOD	JURASSIC PERIOD	
252 mya	201 mya	145 mya

MESOZOIC ERA

RECORD BREAKER

With a head measuring up to 3m (including the frill) – as long as a small car – Pentaceratops has the largest head of any land animal ever.

Viewed from the front, frill makes Pentaceratops look big and scary!

Blood circulating through frill cools quickly, reducing overall body temperature

WHERE TO LOOK?

Head for the western plains of North America, where herds of Pentaceratops roam. With their burly, low-slung bodies and heavy heads, they prefer to graze on low shrubs and branches. They run at quite a pace, however, and once they are moving at speed it takes them a while to stop – so stand well back!

Strong beak-like mouth for ripping plants, rows of teeth in cheeks for chewing

CRETACEOUS PERIOD

66 mya

Now

Late Cretaceous
75–71 million years ago

CENOZOIC ERA

PLATEOSAURUS

Plat-ee-oh-SAW-rus

Name means: Broad lizard

In the Late Triassic, some dinosaurs are trendsetters. Plateosaurus is one of the first herbivores to grow to an enormous size – something that lots more sauropods will do during the Jurassic. That helps it reach more food and keep predators at bay.

DANGER RATING:

3

- Size of a small truck
- Lots of teeth
- Sharp claws

Western Europe

Leans forward as it walks on two legs but can stand more erect

TRIASSIC PERIOD	JURASSIC PERIOD	
252 mya	201 mya	145 mya

Late Triassic
220–205 million years ago

MESOZOIC ERA

Slender head; jaws packed with rough, leaf-shaped teeth, ideal for grinding plant matter

Long neck for reaching high foliage, balanced by long, sturdy tail

WHERE TO LOOK?

Dress for hot weather, as it's almost always dry and warm in the Late Triassic. Scour the plains of what's now northwestern Europe, seeking pockets of forest where Plateosaurus may gather in herds. Some will be nibbling on low shrubs while others rear up to tear at high branches.

SPOTTER STATS

Plant-eater

Length:	5–10m
Weight:	Up to 4 tonnes
Speed:	15km/h
IQ:	Low
Sub-order:	Sauropodomorpha
Family:	Plateosauridae

Swallows gastroliths to help mash plant matter in stomach

Short arms, each with five fingers and three long claws, including a large thumb claw – handy for grabbing branches and fighting off predators

CRETACEOUS PERIOD

66 mya

Now

CENOZOIC ERA

PROTOCERATOPS

Pro-toh-SER-ra-tops

Name means: First horned face

This little relative of Triceratops looks like it has the head of a giant parrot on a lizard's body – with a frill stuck on top for good measure! Small and weird it might be, but it can be fierce when defending itself against predators.

DANGER RATING: 2

- Strong beak
- Sharp teeth
- Fairly small – not much bigger than a sheep

Scurries around on its four slender legs

Mongolia, China

TRIASSIC PERIOD	JURASSIC PERIOD	
252 mya	201 mya	145 mya

MESOZOIC ERA

SPOTTER STATS

Plant-eater

Length:	2.5m
Weight:	175kg
Speed:	24km/h
IQ:	Medium
Order:	Ornithischia
Family:	Protoceratopsidae

Male has larger frill than female, probably to attract mate

WHERE TO LOOK?

Put on a hat and plenty of sunscreen before you head off into eastern Asia's arid scrub. Look in sheltered areas with vegetation, especially near rivers, where these creatures gather in groups and dig burrows for laying eggs. They keep a low profile though and are ever alert for the slightest sign of danger.

Strong, parrot-like beak can rip tough vegetation – and inflict a painful bite

Two pairs of sharp teeth at front of mouth for cutting, rows of squarer teeth at back for munching

CRETACEOUS PERIOD

66 mya

Now

Late Cretaceous
75–71 million years ago

CENOZOIC ERA

PSITTACOSAURUS

Sit-tack-oh-SAW-rus

Name means: Parrot lizard

Small and speedy, these little beaked dinosaurs seek safety in numbers. Scurrying around in gangs, they use their beaks to snip off twigs and leaves, then rush back to their burrows before any big meat-eaters can close in.

Toothless beak covered in hard material called keratin

Distinctive ridge above eye and short bony horns jutting out from cheeks

DANGER RATING:

2

- Strong beak
- Sharp claws
- About the size of a big dog

No teeth for chewing, so swallows gastroliths to mash food in stomach

Mongolia, China, Russia

Arms shorter than legs; as it grows, Psittacosaurus changes from four-legged to two-legged running

TRIASSIC PERIOD	JURASSIC PERIOD	
252 mya	201 mya	145 mya

MESOZOIC ERA

RECORD BREAKER

Psittacosaurus has more babies at one time than any other dinosaur – 34 is the most discovered so far. It's also the best-known dinosaur of all, with hundreds of fossilised skeletons having been found.

WHERE TO LOOK?

It's hot and dusty in Early Cretaceous East Asia, so wear sun protection and drink plenty of water. Try to follow groups of Psittacosaurus to their burrows – if you time it right you might see them tending broods of tiny babies as they first emerge into daylight.

Long quills growing from tail, used for display

SPOTTER STATS

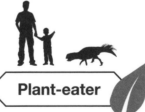

Plant-eater

Length:	1m
Weight:	6kg
Speed:	Up to 40km/h
IQ:	Medium
Order:	Ornithischia
Family:	Psittacosauridae

CRETACEOUS PERIOD

66 mya   Now

Early Cretaceous
125–105 million years ago

CENOZOIC ERA

PTERANODON
Teh-ran-oh-DON

Name means: Winged and toothless

Look up there! Is it a bird or a plane? No, it's a Pteranodon, a giant pterosaur. With a wingspan of up to 10m, these high-flying reptiles are almost as big as a small aircraft and soar in huge flocks across North American skies.

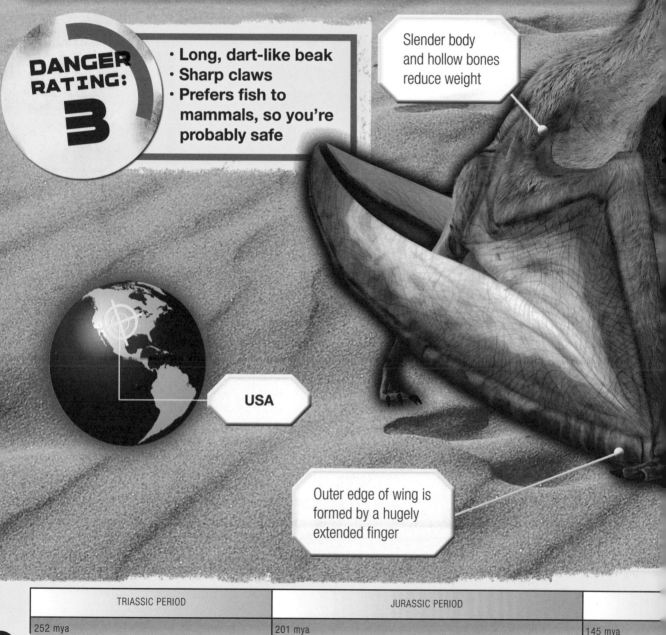

DANGER RATING:

3

- Long, dart-like beak
- Sharp claws
- Prefers fish to mammals, so you're probably safe

Slender body and hollow bones reduce weight

USA

Outer edge of wing is formed by a hugely extended finger

TRIASSIC PERIOD	JURASSIC PERIOD	
252 mya	201 mya	145 mya

MESOZOIC ERA

Big crest, as long as its skull, used for attracting mates and possibly to assist steering in flight

SPOTTER STATS

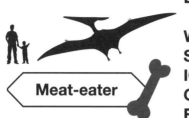

Meat-eater

Length:	2m body, up to 10m wingspan
Weight:	Up to 25kg
Speed:	40km/h
IQ:	Medium
Order:	Pterosauria
Family:	Pteranodontidae

Long, sharply pointed beak with no teeth – food is swallowed whole

WHERE TO LOOK?

Head for the southern shores of the Western Interior Seaway, which covers central North America in the Cretaceous. Pteranodons won't be hard to spot as they're big and there are lots of them. Watch for them swooping down to scoop fish out of the water, or walking awkwardly along the ground with their wings folded.

To take off, Pteranodon runs, 'pole vaults' upwards with its forelimbs and starts flapping

Enormous wings formed by leathery membranes, 5–10m wide on a male, up to 4m wide for a female

CRETACEOUS PERIOD

Late Cretaceous
85–75 million years ago

66 mya

CENOZOIC ERA

Now

QUETZALCOATLUS

Ket-zal-KWAT-lus

Name means: Reference to Aztec feathered serpent god Quetzalcoatl

If you're strolling through the Late Cretaceous woodlands and a giant shadow passes over you, run for cover! It could be this gigantic meat-eating pterosaur, which hunts over land and swoops to seize animals as big as ... well ... you!

Enormous head, up to 2.5m long, and long neck, up to 3m long – both longer than any other pterosaur

DANGER RATING: 8

- Gigantic – and it can fly!
- Massive, strong beak
- Runs fast too!

Air cavities in bones make body light – the weight of just four men

USA, Canada

TRIASSIC PERIOD	JURASSIC PERIOD	
252 mya	201 mya	145 mya

MESOZOIC ERA

WHERE TO LOOK?

Keep watch for its massive winged form soaring overhead. But bear in mind too that it can also land and stalk prey through forests, dashing out from dense trees or simply darting its huge beak forwards to snap up small reptiles and mammals.

Outer edge of wing is formed by a hugely extended finger

Can walk and run on all fours; when on ground looks like a giraffe with wings!

Membranes stretch between bones to form massive wings; stiff fibres inside membranes maintain shape and permit folding

SPOTTER STATS

Omnivore

Length:	9m body, up to 11m wingspan
Weight:	250kg
Speed:	Up to 130km/h
IQ:	Medium to high
Order:	Pterosauria
Family:	Azhdarchidae

CRETACEOUS PERIOD

Late Cretaceous
70–66 million years ago

66 mya

CENOZOIC ERA

Now

SAUROPOSEIDON

Saw-row-poh-SIDE-un

Name means: Earthquake god lizard

If you were sitting on the sixth floor of a building, this guy could walk past and peer in the window. Its phenomenally long neck allows it to reach a height of 18m and feast on foods beyond the reach of any other dinosaur.

DANGER RATING: 4

- Gargantuan!
- Massive legs and feet could crush you to a pulp
- Swinging tail could knock you out

Hollow cavities in neck bones make neck lighter

Swallows gastroliths to help mash up tough plant food in stomach and aid digestion

USA

High, pillar-like legs and massive, broad feet provide firm foundations

TRIASSIC PERIOD	JURASSIC PERIOD	
252 mya	201 mya	145 mya

MESOZOIC ERA

Small head with ridged brows

WHERE TO LOOK?

This massive sauropod inhabits the swampy shores of the Gulf of Mexico. It's not called the 'earthquake god lizard' for nothing, so the ground really is likely to shake as it approaches! Look up and you could see its slender head and neck curling through the treetops to snack on the highest branches.

RECORD BREAKER

Sauroposeidon is the tallest dinosaur ever. It is also phenomenally heavy, weighing as much as 10 male African elephants.

Additional bony rods called neck ribs provide extra support, helping hold neck and head erect

SPOTTER STATS

Plant-eater

Length:	27m
Weight:	40–50 tonnes
Speed:	16km/h
IQ:	Low
Sub-order:	Sauropodomorpha
Clade:	Titanosauriformes

CRETACEOUS PERIOD

66 mya

Now

Early Cretaceous
115–105 million years ago

CENOZOIC ERA

SHANTUNGOSAURUS

Shan-toon-go-SAW-rus

Name means: Lizard from Shandong (in China, where fossils were discovered)

Aside from the sauropods, this is possibly the heaviest dinosaur of all time. It's an amazing sight as it lumbers along on all fours and completely astounding when it rears up on its back legs to stand as tall as a two-storey house!

DANGER RATING:

4

- **Gigantic**
- **Big strong jaw**
- **Herds can be a major hazard**

Large, long head with wide, duckbill-shaped mouth

Toothless hard beak at front of jaw for ripping off foliage, hundreds of teeth at back for grinding it up

RECORD BREAKER

Almost 17m long and as heavy as three African elephants, Shantungosaurus is the biggest duckbilled dinosaur, or hadrosaur, of all time. Among non-sauropods it is pipped in length by Spinosaurus.

China

TRIASSIC PERIOD	JURASSIC PERIOD	
252 mya	201 mya	145 mya

MESOZOIC ERA

SPOTTER STATS

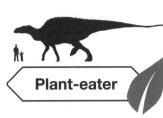

Plant-eater

Length:	16.5m
Weight:	15 tonnes
Speed:	24km/h
IQ:	Low
Order:	Ornithischia
Family:	Hadrosauridae

Front legs about 2m high, back legs a whopping 4m tall – about the height of two very tall humans stood on top of each other

Massive body held horizontally; long tail balances heavy neck and head

WHERE TO LOOK?

Given its size, Shantungosaurus shouldn't be hard to spot in the East Asian forests. Even if hidden by foliage it's likely to make quite a racket as it crashes through the trees, flattening everything in its path. If you see a herd of these herbivores running towards you, step aside fast!

CRETACEOUS PERIOD

66 mya

Now

Late Cretaceous
100–70 million years ago

CENOZOIC ERA

SHONISAURUS

Show-nee-SAW-rus

Name means: Lizard from the Shoshone Mountains (in Nevada, USA, where fossils were first found)

This massive sea creature is as big as a small submarine – if it had a door in it, you could easily climb inside. One of the largest ocean-going reptiles of all time, it need only open its mouth to swallow up human-size squid and fish.

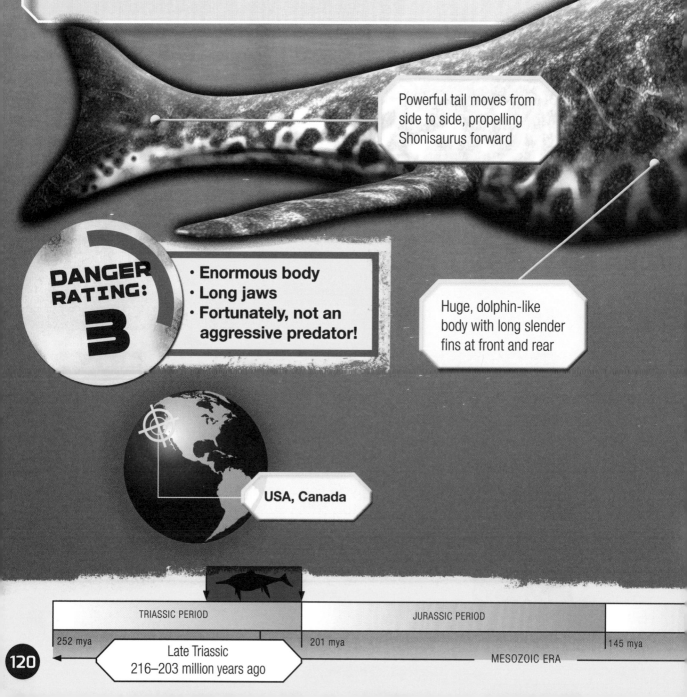

Powerful tail moves from side to side, propelling Shonisaurus forward

DANGER RATING: 3

- Enormous body
- Long jaws
- Fortunately, not an aggressive predator!

Huge, dolphin-like body with long slender fins at front and rear

USA, Canada

TRIASSIC PERIOD	JURASSIC PERIOD	
252 mya	201 mya	145 mya

Late Triassic
216–203 million years ago

MESOZOIC ERA

WHERE TO LOOK?

Like other marine reptiles, Shonisaurus has to surface regularly to breathe. Climb a high cliff and scan the sea with binoculars and you may spot its great head and back breaking the surface – a spectacular sight!

Long jaws of adults do not have teeth, so Shonisaurus simply grabs then swallows softer creatures, such as squid

Large eyes allow Shonisaurus to spot prey in deep, murky water

Each fin is up to 3m long and made of many disc-shaped finger bones

SPOTTER STATS

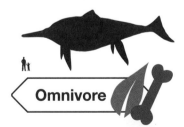

Omnivore

Length:	15m
Weight:	20 tonnes
Speed:	Up to 15km/h
IQ:	Low
Order:	Ichthyosauria
Family:	Shastasauridae

CRETACEOUS PERIOD

66 mya

Now

CENOZOIC ERA

SHUVUUIA

Shoo-VOO-ya

Name means: Bird, in Mongolian

You probably know a few, and the age of dinosaurs had them too: fussy eaters. Shuvuuia, for instance, will eat nothing but insects. As a result, it has developed special tools for getting to its favourite foods – huge, curved thumb claws that can crack open an insect nest in seconds.

Large eyes help locate tiny insects

DANGER RATING:

1

- Large claws on feet
- Big, pointed thumb claws
- Small and eats only insects

Enormous thumb with hooked claw used to open up insect nests

Mongolia

WHERE TO LOOK?

Carry plenty of water and wear sun protection as you search for this speedy, bird-like dino in the Mongolian desert. Look for piles of dead wood or mounds of earth made by termites and you might just catch Shuvuuia hard at work, digging deep for food.

TRIASSIC PERIOD	JURASSIC PERIOD	
252 mya	201 mya	145 mya

MESOZOIC ERA

Feathers sprout from head, tail and arms

Light body, strong back legs and long tail all help Shuvuuia speed along and escape predators

Soft fur covers body, neck and legs, helping Shuvuuia stay warm on cold desert nights

Two smaller fingers concealed by feathers, possibly used for grooming

SPOTTER STATS

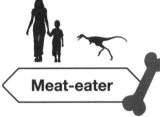

Meat-eater

Length:	0.6m
Weight:	3.5kg
Speed:	48km/h
IQ:	High
Sub-order:	Theropoda
Family:	Alvarezsauridae

CRETACEOUS PERIOD

66 mya

Now

Late Cretaceous
84–74 million years ago

CENOZOIC ERA

SPINOSAURUS

Spine-oh-SAW-rus

Name means: Thorn lizard

No doubt about it, Spinosaurus is one of the scariest-looking animals of all time. This fearsome predator is even bigger than Tyrannosaurus and can run almost as fast. With a colourful crest running the length of its spine, it's hard to miss!

DANGER RATING: 10

- **Huge, hooked claws**
- **Jaws like a crocodile**
- **Fast – can run 100m in 11–12 seconds**

Huge, colourful sail along its back – used to control body temperature, attract a mate or scare off rivals

Egypt, Morocco

Walks on two muscular back legs most of the time, and sometimes on all fours

TRIASSIC PERIOD	JURASSIC PERIOD	
252 mya	201 mya	145 mya

MESOZOIC ERA

Binocular vision helps judge distance and time attacks on large fish

Long teeth at the front of the mouth mesh together to trap slippery fish

RECORD BREAKER

Spinosaurus is thought to be the biggest predator ever to walk on two legs! It's almost twice as long as a bus and as heavy as two African elephants.

Giant head, as long as a fully grown man, at 1.8m

WHERE TO LOOK?

Pull on your wellington boots and head for North Africa's lagoons and swamps, where Spinosaurus likes to wade into the water to spear fish. Track it and you might also see it scavenging on dead creatures. But make sure you keep a low profile – you really don't want to catch this guy's eye!

Three claws on each hand, good for spearing fish, especially the large thumb

SPOTTER STATS

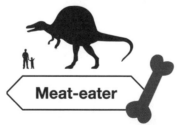

Meat-eater

Length:	Up to 18m
Weight:	10 tonnes
Speed:	32km/h
IQ:	High
Sub-order:	Theropod
Family:	Spinosauridae

CRETACEOUS PERIOD

66 mya

Now

Early to Late Cretaceous 112–95 million years ago

CENOZOIC ERA

STEGOSAURUS
Steg-oh-SAW-rus

Name means: Plated lizard

You probably already know this guy, one of the most famous and recognisable dinosaurs of all time. But although that spectacular arrangement of plates along its back is familiar, we still aren't sure what the plates do. Can you find out?

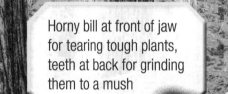

Horny bill at front of jaw for tearing tough plants, teeth at back for grinding them to a mush

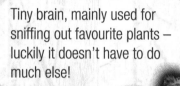

Tiny brain, mainly used for sniffing out favourite plants – luckily it doesn't have to do much else!

DANGER RATING: 5

- Big and heavy
- May stampede if frightened
- Long, sharp spines on tail

RECORD BREAKER

Not the brightest spark, Stegosaurus is known to have the smallest brain of any dinosaur. The part used for thinking is as small as a walnut. Your brain is about 25 times as big!

USA, Portugal

TRIASSIC PERIOD	JURASSIC PERIOD	
252 mya	201 mya	145 mya

MESOZOIC ERA

Late Jurassic
154–145 million years ago

Two rows of horn-covered bony plates along back, some up to 70cm tall and 80cm wide

WHERE TO LOOK?

A slow-mover, Stegosaurus relies on its large size and spiky tail to deter predators. So it doesn't hide away and is therefore easy to find. Look for it in forest clearings, where it likes to munch on low-growing plants such as ferns – lots of them!

Plates of little use for defence, so probably for controlling body temperature (by absorbing and releasing heat), identification or showing off to potential mates

Two pairs of sharp spikes on tail, each up to 1m long – Stegosaurus's best form of defence

SPOTTER STATS

Plant-eater

Length:	7m
Weight:	3.5 tonnes
Speed:	16km/h
IQ:	Low
Order:	Ornithischia
Family:	Stegosauridae

CRETACEOUS PERIOD

66 mya   Now

CENOZOIC ERA

STRUTHIOMIMUS

Strooth-ee-oh-MIME-us

Name means: Ostrich mimic

And they're off! Imagine a running race between every kind of dinosaur. This ostrich-like creature would be a clear favourite to win. With its powerful legs and giant stride, it can speed along almost as fast as a car on a motorway.

Big tail helps with balance and sudden changes of direction – great for shaking off pesky predators!

Muscular thighs help legs move quickly

DANGER RATING: 2

- **About twice your size**
- **Sharp claws**
- **Could run you over if you get in its way**

At full speed, only its toe tips touch the ground and a single stride can stretch 9m!

USA, Canada

TRIASSIC PERIOD	JURASSIC PERIOD	
252 mya	201 mya	145 mya

MESOZOIC ERA

RECORD BREAKER

Struthiomimus is the fastest dinosaur of all time, beating rivals like Gallimimus by quite some way. Going full tilt, it can clock up more than 60km/h.

Small head, slender neck and slim arms make upper body light

WHERE TO LOOK?

When moving at top speed, Struthiomimus will be a bit of a blur. Try to sneak up on it as it feeds on shrubs or gathers insects and seeds from the ground. But if you startle it or there's any other sign of danger – whoosh! – it's gone!

Long, curved hand claws useful for pulling down branches to strip off leaves and seeds with long beak

SPOTTER STATS

Omnivore

Length:	4m
Weight:	150kg
Speed:	More than 60km/h
IQ:	High
Sub-order:	Theropoda
Family:	Ornithomimidae

CRETACEOUS PERIOD

66 mya

Now

Late Cretaceous
70–66 million years ago

CENOZOIC ERA

THERIZINOSAURUS

Thair-ee-zine-oh-SAW-rus

Name means: Scythe lizard

Even the biggest, meanest predator will hesitate before tussling with something as huge and weird as Therizinosaurus. And when it sees those colossal claws – like six sharp swords – it might just decide to turn and run.

DANGER RATING: 4

- Gigantic
- Six huge sharp claws
- Lucky for you, it eats only insects and leaves

Each of the claws on Therizinosaurus's hands was at least 70cm long – the longest of any animal ever.

Wide, rounded body and short tail, covered in feathers that keep it warm

Mongolia

Broad feet with strong toes and hooked claws support great weight

TRIASSIC PERIOD	JURASSIC PERIOD	
252 mya	201 mya	145 mya

MESOZOIC ERA

Small head with broad beak, toothless at the front but lined further back with small leaf-shaped teeth for chewing plants

Long, giraffe-like neck helps reach high trees

Giant claws deter predators and also useful for pulling high branches down towards mouth

WHERE TO LOOK?

Wander the sparse Mongolian woodlands and look for big trees shaking. That could well be Therizinosaurus pulling branches down with its large claws to strip off leaves and berries. Despite its alarming appearance, it's unlikely to attack unless you get very close.

SPOTTER STATS

Omnivore

Length:	8m
Weight:	5 tonnes
Speed:	32km/h
IQ:	Medium
Sub-order:	Theropoda
Family:	Therizinosauridae

CRETACEOUS PERIOD

66 mya

Now

Late Cretaceous
70–66 million years ago

CENOZOIC ERA

TRICERATOPS

Try-SEH-ra-tops

Name means: Horrible three-horned face

When Tyrannosaurus is one of your near neighbours, you need all the protection you can get! Rhino-like Triceratops's tough hide, sturdy skull and enormous frill shield it from bites and scratches, while its spear-like horns become deadly weapons when thrust at attackers.

DANGER RATING:

4

- Almost as big as a bus
- Huge sharp horns
- Strong jaw

Huge frill provides protection but also used to show off to rivals and attract mates

Large, bulky body and short, sturdy legs

USA, Canada

TRIASSIC PERIOD		JURASSIC PERIOD	
252 mya		201 mya	145 mya

MESOZOIC ERA

Brow horns can be up to 1m long, with very sharp points; used to fight rivals as well as predators

WHERE TO LOOK?

Take the utmost care here in the kingdom of Tyrannosaurus! Look for small groups of Triceratops in clearings, grazing on low-growing plants, usually early or late in the day so they are harder for predators to find. In forested areas, you might see one using its massive bulk to bulldoze taller plants to the ground, so that it can feed on their foliage too.

Strong, horny beak for ripping out foliage; rows of teeth at back of mouth (up to 800 in all!) grind plants to a mush

Massive frill up to 1m wide and made of solid bone

SPOTTER STATS

Omnivore

Length:	9m
Weight:	5.5 tonnes
Speed:	20km/h
IQ:	Low
Order:	Ornithischia
Family:	Ceratopsidae

CRETACEOUS PERIOD

66 mya

Now

Late Cretaceous
68–66 million years ago

CENOZOIC ERA

TROODON
TROO-oh-don

Name means: Wounding tooth

Don't let that daffy expression fool you: this dino is a clever clogs. Its much-larger-than-average brain makes it a highly effective hunter, able to spot and sniff out the tiniest creatures and appreciate the benefits of eating fruit, eggs and seeds too.

DANGER RATING:
4

- Fast and agile
- Sharp claws on hands and feet
- Prefers prey smaller than you, unless already dead

Long, beak-like snout with small, sharp, serrated teeth – great for chopping small animals as well as leaves and fruit

USA, Canada

WHERE TO LOOK?

Troodons stalk through the forests of western North America, foraging for food. If you spot one, try to follow it and you could see it pouncing on prey such as baby hadrosaurs. You might also track it back to its nest, a dish-shaped hollow in the dirt where it lays up to 24 unusual, elongated eggs.

TRIASSIC PERIOD	JURASSIC PERIOD	
252 mya	201 mya	145 mya

MESOZOIC ERA

Forward-facing eyes combine with large brain to provide sharp sight

SPOTTER STATS

Omnivore

Length:	2.5m
Weight:	35kg
Speed:	48km/h
IQ:	High
Sub-order:	Theropoda
Family:	Troodontidae

Covering of short feathers keeps body warm

RECORD BREAKER

Relative to its size, Troodon has the biggest brain of any dinosaur and so is probably the smartest. Not that it's about to help you with your homework – it's only about as clever as a modern chicken.

Strong legs for running fast and long tail to help balance

Big, curved claw on second toe, useful for ripping up prey; turned upwards when it runs

CRETACEOUS PERIOD

66 mya

Now

Late Cretaceous
70–66 million years ago

CENOZOIC ERA

TYRANNOSAURUS
Tie-ran-oh-SAW-rus

Name means: Tyrant lizard

Though not the biggest meat-eater, Tyrannosaurus is the undisputed king of the dinosaur world, the most famous predator of all and a superstar of films, documentaries and museum displays. Movie-star looks certainly play a part, but it's mainly down to its fearsome reputation as a ferocious, merciless killer.

DANGER RATING: 10

- Massive head and jaws
- Huge, dagger-like teeth
- Bone-crunching bite – help!

Long, thick tail held straight out to balance forward lean of upper body

SPOTTER STATS

Meat-eater

Length:	12m
Weight:	6 tonnes
Speed:	29km/h
IQ:	High
Sub-order:	Theropoda
Family:	Tyrannosauridae

USA, Canada

TRIASSIC PERIOD	JURASSIC PERIOD	
252 mya	201 mya	145 mya

MESOZOIC ERA

Roof of mouth, made of thick, hard bone, reinforces powerful bite

Colossal head with hugely powerful jaws containing 58 teeth, each one up to 18cm (up to 30cm including root)

Huge shoulder muscles support large head and provide extra flesh-ripping power

Tiny arms with two long, sharp claws on each, used mainly for holding struggling prey

WHERE TO LOOK?

Stalking the world's deadliest predator through western American forests is a risky business. With its heightened sense of smell, Tyrannosaurus could quickly sniff you out from afar. Creep cautiously and always be ready to scurry up a very high tree or dodge through dense undergrowth to shake it off.

CRETACEOUS PERIOD

66 mya

Now

Late Cretaceous
67–66 million years ago

CENOZOIC ERA

UTAHRAPTOR

You-tah-RAP-tor

Name means: Robber from Utah (state in USA where fossils were first found)

It's not the biggest but this is definitely one of the scariest Cretaceous predators. With its powerful jaws, serrated teeth, razor-sharp front claws and two long, hooked foot claws for finishing off its victims, Utahraptor is a terrifyingly efficient killing machine.

DANGER RATING: 9

- Much bigger than you, and very fast
- Large jaws lined with sharp teeth
- Knife-like claws

USA

Sharp, hooked claws on hands and feet, used to stab and cling onto prey

TRIASSIC PERIOD	JURASSIC PERIOD	
252 mya	201 mya	Early Cretaceous 124–128 million years ago

MESOZOIC ERA

SPOTTER STATS

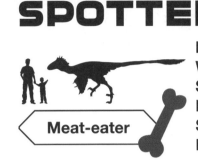

Meat-eater

Length:	7m
Weight:	700kg
Speed:	48km/h
IQ:	High
Sub-order:	Theropoda
Family:	Dromaeosauridae

WHERE TO LOOK?

Western American woodlands are the main haunt of Utahraptor. Find a safe vantage point from which to watch this hunter in action, such as a tall tree. Meeting one Utahraptor would be bad enough, but it's thought that these guys also hunt in packs – a horrifying prospect!

Bony rods growing out of the tail bones keep the tail stiff and in turn improve balance

Relatively short, muscular legs power bursts of high speed when pursuing prey or fleeing predators

Long feathers grow out of arms and tail, possibly helping camouflage Utahraptor in forest

Huge sickle-shaped claw on second toe of foot, up to 25cm long, can stab and slice

VELOCIRAPTOR

Veh-loss-ee-RAP-tor

Name means: Swift stealer

Feathered, fast and fearless, this pint-sized predator packs a lethal punch – usually delivered by one of its big, sharp, sickle-shaped foot claws. Don't let its small stature catch you off guard – keep away!

Stiff tail is held high to assist balance when running or kicking prey

DANGER RATING: 7

- **Fast mover**
- **Sharp claws**
- **Big jaws with lots of spiky teeth**

Hugely enlarged, sickle-shaped claw on second toe of each foot, Velociraptor's deadliest weapon

Mongolia, China, Russia

TRIASSIC PERIOD	JURASSIC PERIOD	
252 mya	201 mya	145 mya

MESOZOIC ERA

Eyes adapted for hunting in low light

Distinctive long, slightly upturned snout

Long jaws packed with up to 60 small, sharp teeth designed for tearing flesh

WHERE TO LOOK?

Velociraptor hunts on the open plains and rolling dunes of the arid East Asian interior, attacking small mammals and dinosaurs as big, and sometimes bigger, than itself.

Short feathers cover most of body, longer ones sprout from arms and tail

SPOTTER STATS

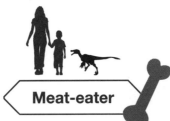

Meat-eater

Length:	2m
Weight:	7–15kg
Speed:	40km/h
IQ:	High
Sub-order:	Theropoda
Family:	Dromaeosauridae

CRETACEOUS PERIOD

Late Cretaceous
75–71 million years ago

66 mya

Now

CENOZOIC ERA

GLOSSARY

ANKYLOSAURS: A group of large plant-eating dinosaurs that lived in North America and Asia during the Late Cretaceous. Their heads, backs and tails were usually covered with bony, armour-like plates and spikes.

CARNIVORE: An animal that eats only or mainly meat – other animals, in other words.

CERATOPSIANS: A group of mostly large, rhino-like, plant-eating dinosaurs that lived in North America and Asia in the Late Cretaceous. They had heads with large frills, beak-like mouths, and, usually, long horns. Triceratops is the best-known ceratopsian.

CLADE: A group of animals that share body features and a common ancestor.

CLASS: A major category of animals, such as birds, reptiles or mammals, as used in traditional classification.

COPROLITE: A fossilised dinosaur poo.

CRETACEOUS: The third period of the Mesozoic Era, from 145 to 66 million years ago, which had the largest number of kinds of dinosaurs but ended with a mass extinction.

EVOLUTION: The biological process by which living things gradually change as they adapt to suit their environment.

EXTINCTION: The end of a particular kind, or species, of animal, when the last of its kind dies.

FAMILY: A group to which several species with shared characteristics belong.

FOSSIL: A trace of a prehistoric plant or animal, preserved as stone or as an impression in rock.

GASTROLITH: Any stone that an animal swallows to help it break down food in its stomach.

GENUS: A group of very closely related species, or type of animal, that share the same name. Tyrannosaurus is a genus name, and Tyrannosaurus rex is a species that belongs to that genus.

HADROSAUR: A group of large, plant-eating, duckbilled dinosaurs that lived in Asia, Europe and the Americas during the Cretaceous Period.

HERBIVORE: An animal that eats only plants, not meat.

ICHTHYOSAURS: A group of dolphin-shaped marine reptiles that lived at the same time as the dinosaurs.

JURASSIC: The second period of the Mesozoic Era, from 201 to 145 million years ago, when there were lots of giant sauropods around.

MAMMALS: A group of animals that have backbones, are covered with hair or fur and feed milk to their babies. Humans are mammals.

MESOZOIC ERA: The span of time from 252 to 66 million years ago, during which the dinosaurs emerged, thrived and died. It is divided into the Triassic, Jurassic and Cretaceous periods.

OMNIVORE: An animal that eats all kinds of foods, including meat and plant matter.

ORDERS: The major groups of a kind of animal. Dinosaurs are divided into two main orders, the ornithischians and saurischians.

ORNITHISCHIANS: One of the two major groups of dinosaurs, distinguished by the shape of their pubic bone, part of the hips or pelvis. The ornithischians had a pubic bone that pointed backwards, like those of birds, and so are also called bird-hipped dinosaurs. Most ornithischians were plant-eaters.

PALAEONTOLOGIST: A scientist who studies prehistoric forms of life, including dinosaurs.

PLESIOSAURS: A group of large, long-necked marine reptiles that lived at the same time as the dinosaurs.

PLIOSAURS: A group of large, short-necked marine reptiles that lived at the same time as the dinosaurs.

PREDATOR: A meat-eating animal that hunts and kills other animals.

PTEROSAURS: A group of flying reptiles that lived at the same time as the dinosaurs, whose wings were formed by stretched sheets of skin.

SAURISCHIANS: One of the two major groups of dinosaurs, distinguished by the shape of their pubic bone, part of the hips or pelvis. The saurischians had a pubic bone that pointed downwards and forwards, like those of lizards, and so are also called lizard-hipped dinosaurs. The saurischians included plant-eaters and meat-eaters.

SAUROPODS: A group of large, long-necked plant-eating dinosaurs, some of which were the largest land animals of all time.

SCAVENGER: An animal that feeds partly or mainly on creatures that are already dead, or scraps left by other animals.

SERRATED: Having jagged edges, like the teeth on a saw.

SPECIES: A type of plants and animals that have the same body features and can breed together. A group of closely related species make up a genus. The species Tyrannosaurus rex, for example, is part of the Tyrannosaurus genus.

STEGOSAURS: A group of large, four-legged, plant-eating dinosaurs, which had rows of vertical plates running along their backs. Stegosaurus is the best-known stegosaur.

SUB-ORDER: A category of dinosaurs between order and family – a bit like an extended family group. The theropods and sauropods are sub-orders of the saurischian order in the traditional classification of dinosaurs.

THEROPODS: A group of meat-eating saurischian dinosaurs that usually walked on their hind legs. Among the best-known theropods are Tyrannosaurus and Velociraptor.

TRIASSIC: The first period of the Mesozoic Era, from 252 to 201 million years ago, during which dinosaurs first appeared.

VERTEBRAE: The bones that join together to form an animal's spine, running from the head to the tail.

THIS IS A CARLTON BOOK

© Carlton Books Limited 2015

Editor: Tasha Percy
Designer: Dani Lurie
Packager: Solas Text and Design
Consultant: Douglas Palmer
Production: Charlotte Cade

Published in 2015 by Carlton Books Ltd
An imprint of the Carlton Publishing Group
20 Mortimer Street, London W1T 3JW

10 9 8 7 6 5 4 3 2 1

A catalogue record for this book is available from the
British Library.

ISBN: 978-1-78312-113-7

Printed in Dubai